An Introduction to the Science and Art of Selling.
2nd Edition

Written by Michael Bonilla

Table of Contents

About the Author 16

Preface..19

Chapter 1: Introduction 23

Why'd I write this book?...................................25

Why do you want to be a salesperson?........26

What is selling?..27

What is Influence?...28

What is Persuasion?..29

What do you do really well?...........................30

Why should everyone learn to sell?..............31

Limited Information Game 32

Different Types of Salespeople......................32

What makes a great salesman? 35

Opening a sale vs Closing a sale 36

Knowledge is Power..37

Find a Mentor 38

How do I go about getting a mentor?...............38

Why should I get a mentor? 39

Mentoring Misconceptions.................................39

Embedding 40

   Author Example: Embedding...............................41

Sell Me This 'Pen' 42

What's the difference between a novice and pro? 44

Selling Statistics..45

Don't give up to easily. In sales, people will say no, people will say yes and people will say maybe. 48

Should you leave a message when cold calling?..49

Top Five Rules of Success in Sales.................52

   1. Have a Process...52

   2. Network Every Day...................................52

   3. Follow Up...52

   4. Don't instantly give up if someone says no.

   5. Read about your industry for 30 minutes every day. 53

What does a Salesman do? Why do we need them?..54

Increasing Your Odds......................................55

Challenges Facing Modern Salespeople 57

Consumer Advertisement Bombardment

    Oversaturation...58

Hyper-Competitive Price Environment...............59

General Expertise / Jack of All Trade Syndrome

Sales Stigma 62

Sales Aversion 63

Two Most Common Questions from New

    Salespeople 65

Understanding the Sales Funnel 65

Leads...66

Prospecting 68

Appointments...70

Presentations 70

Sales...71

Understanding Learning...................................72

4 levels of learning 72

How Long Does it Take to Master A Skill?........74

The Cone of Learning...74

Glen Gary Glen Ross as a critique on sales

    culture. 77

Chapter 2: Networking & Prospecting 80

Networking versus Prospecting 81

What is the Goal of Networking? 81

What is the Goal of Prospecting? 81

What prospecting is and is not. 82

First Impressions and Prospecting/Networking 82

Four Pillars of Human Conversation 84

Example: Using Tesla 85

Rapport Building Processes 86

Other Rapport Prospecting Questions................86

Find out what a person is reading. 87

Rapport Building..87

Clearing Out a Room 90

Unique Value Proposition – UVP 91

Developing Your Unique Value Proposition......92

Follow Up On Social Media 92

Note from Author 93

Don't Overthink Networking............................94

Networking is not a competition. 94

Networking Buddies – Dynamic Duo 95

Throw Out a Line 95

Incidental Similarities 96

Networking Mistakes **97**

Unrealistic Expectations Going Into an Event.

Not Playing the Numbers 98

Not Following Up 99

A Too Casual Approach 100

Lack of Specificity 100

Patience is a Virtue 101

Talking too much About You 101

Showing Up Unprepared 102

Properly Dealing with Gatekeepers **103**

Finding the Decision Maker **105**

Chapter 3: Understanding Consumer Psychology and Buying Behavior **106**

Types of Consumers **108**

Have you flushed out their belief systems?

Framing a Question **110**

Feel vs Think people **111**

A simple example. 112

How do you identify feel people?.....................113

How do you identify think people?...................113

Why do People buy things? 113

Understanding Consumer Segmentation 114

1. Geographical..114

2. Demographic...114

3. Behavioral 115

4. Psychographic 115

Why should we Segment?...............................115

Consumer Life Stages.....................................116

Space invaders 118

Space Invader Exercise 118

Why do I need an online presence?...............119

Why Consumers Appreciate Customization 122

Author Example 122

Chapter 4: Mental Game of a Salesman............123

Mentality of a Salesman 124

External Activities to Increase Sales Skills.125

Focus on what you can control.......................126

Control your language. 128

What motivates you? 129

tutto finisce 130

Time Management is everything. 130

    Be authentic 131

    Time as an Investment 132

    Firstly, time block. 133

    Secondly, Learn to Schedule your Calendar out.

    Third, find time to confirm. 134

    Lastly, write down your to-do list. 135

Why do most Salespeople fail? 135

The Power of Self-affirmation 136

Commitment 137

Chapter 5: Cross Selling and Upselling 138

Cross Selling 139

Up Selling 140

Don't leave Money on the Table 141

Up-selling: Waitress Example 142

Amazon Cross Selling System 143

Don't Spend the Clients Money for Them 144

Up-Selling/Cross-Selling: Don't spend the client's money for them.................145

What Percentage of your prospects do you try to cross sell?.................147

What can Upselling do for my Income? 148

Chapter 6: Objections.................149

What is an objection?.................151

Why do prospects talk to salespeople?........151

Tension Threshold Principle.................152

Why do people object?.................153

Underlying uncertainty.................154

How to categorize objections. 155

Identifying a Complaint and Identifying an Objection.................157

How to determine the root cause of an objection? 158

Flush Objections Out at the Onset 158

Understanding Common Objections Consumers Use.................160

Price is a surface level objection.................162

Understanding how to Pre-empt and flush out Objections. 167

Example # 1: I need to talk to my spouse......169

Example #2: I don't have the time right now...

Example #3: "I've read some bad reviews (online) about that company." 172

Have a Process for Handling Objections......173

Complaints vs Objections...............................176

Chapter 7: Soft Skills 177

What are soft skills? 179

- Observation 179

- Relative Disassociation 179

- Caring 179

- Charisma..179

- Dispute Resolution...............................179

- Conversationalist-ism..........................179

Strategic Pausing...180

Matching and Mirroring 181

Learn to Smile 182

Desirable Soft Skills for Salespeople............182

Charisma 183

Dispute Resolution 183

Actively Listening 185

The Art of Showmanship 186

Reading a Client (Non-Verbal Cues).............**186**

Developing Sales and Soft Skills.......................187

Empathy 188

Tonality...188

Chapter 8: Goals **189**

Two Types of Goals..**191**

- Activity Goal: 192

- Result (sales) Goal:...................................192

Stretch Goals and Incrementalism................**193**

Goals Incremental and Vision Monumental 194

How to set S.M.A.R.T goals? **194**

Specific 195

Measurable 195

Attainable 195

Relevant 196

Timely 196

Let's set some Goals!.....................................197

Goal Reinforcement.................................198

Mistakes Often Associated with Goal Setting

Lack of Goal Visibility 201

Setting Too Many Goals 202

Setting Goals Too High.............................202

Confusing a Goal for a Vision 203

Setting Goals without a baseline 203

Lack of Prioritization................................204

Guilt by Association...................................205

Distracted Driving 205

Chapter 9: Selling as a Process......................206

What will mastering a process do for me?..209

Getting on Base. 210

Don't leap into your shtick.......................210

Setting and Managing Expectations 211

Telling isn't selling....................................212

What does this client care about? 213

QERC Simple System...............................214

The power of planting seeds 216

Rapidly Identify High Intent Leads...............216

Talking in Future Tense 217

Prospecting 218

How many cold calls should I make per day?

Building a cold calling script 219

Designing a Process 221

Theoretical Framework for a Sales Process

Discovery Call (Fact Finding) 223

Problem Identification 225

Sales Call (Presentation) 227

Identifying Buying Questions 229

Closing Strategies 229

But Mike, I don't want to come off as phony by using a standard process... 230

Asking for referrals 231

Check the Rapport 232

Confidence is Key 238

Principle of Reciprocity 239

Chapter 10: Fact Finder 248

Three Core Elements of a Fact Finder 249

Where have you been? 250

Where are you now? 251

Where do you want to go? 251

Purpose of a Fact Finder.................................252

Errors and Omissions.................................253

Focus 253

Memory and Fact Gathering.................................254

Mistakes of Most Fact Finders.................................255

Some Fact Finder Questions 256

Chapter 11: Closing a Sale.................................257

Asking to Ask Asking for permission to ask for the sale. 259

Three Most Common Closing Questions.......259

When do I know a person is ready to be closed?

When should I close? 260

How do I close a sale? 261

How do I determine my Close Ratio?...........262

Closing Strategies 263

Options after the Close. 264

Chapter 12: Follow Up 265

Follow Up Systems 266

Lead Management.................................267

Client Renewal Programs.................................267

Prospect Did Not Sell (DNS) 267

Designing a Follow-Up Process 268

Chapter 13: Sales Ethics................................269

Sales Ethics...270

Developing a Code of Ethics........................271

Core Components of Ethical Selling.............271

Ethical Lens 272

Ethical Decision Making: How do I know? ..273

Summation...274

Index of Questions 276

About the Author

Believe it or not this section is always the hardest for me to write about. I really don't enjoy talking about myself. I enjoy having people talk about themselves. What do people want to know about an author? Background? Experiences? Belief systems? I enjoy breaking things and putting them back together. What kind of person am I? What kind of person do I want to represent?

Let me tell you a brief story that tells you what kind of person I am. Back in the early 90's I was sketching out my design for a boxcar derby car for boy scouts. This was my first race and I couldn't think of the type of car I wanted to build. To say the least there was zero inspiration. I scribbled out some designs on this piece of paper and eventually after running out of paper went into the den to find more paper. I stopped for a second and glanced over by the window. After staring out of the window for a second (maybe several minutes) I saw my father as he was pulling into the driveway with his 1990 White Dodge diesel, you could hear it for miles.

Then it hit me. What if I used his truck as the design? I re-read the instructions and rules for the derby. The boxcar kit came in a small cardboard box with a block of wood we could use to make our cars. The instructions read as follows:

* Must have 4 wheels

* Must weigh X LBs, no more and no less.

* Must be X inches long by X Inches wide.

So, that being said. Nowhere in the rules/instructions did it specifically say "this boxcar must be a car". So, for the first time in the boxcar derby history. Michael Bonilla entered a truck. To which everyone started laughing. It was a small wooded version of a 1990's Dodge Ram 2500. With a big Pepsi decal on the driver side door. So, we called it the Pepsi truck.

I placed my 'car' on the race line for the first race and hoped for the best. The judges looked at it. It met the weight requirements, the size requirements and had the appropriate amount of wheels. So, we raced and I waited with anticipation for the results. As I was short I couldn't even see the race. All I heard was, "Pepsi truck 1st place." After all 5 races that day I kept hearing those same words over and over again.

After sweeping that year's event. The following year I decided to change it up and make a replica of the Mach 5 Speed Racer Car, in which I came in third place. That next year every 'car' was a truck, besides mine. Don't bend the rules, don't break the rules, test the rules and test the boundaries of the game you are given. Look for loopholes and exploits in the system.

I'm unsure what kind of insight that might have provided. Nevertheless, this book is the longest, most through and probably well thought out I have written to date. I'm an author, a consultant, a former agency owner, an avid golfer, a husband and most importantly someone who enjoys giving back through teaching.

Preface

Selling is a lot like playing Texas Hold'em. Poker is classified as a limited information game and each hand has an implied odds of winning or losing. Poker, like selling, is also a zero sum game in which one player will win and one player will lose. The ultimate goal of a salesperson is to sell and persuade a qualified consumer to buy.

In poker, a limited information game, as you progress thru your hand more cards are revealed, which helps you make a more informed decision. As the game progresses other players also reveal information about the strength of their hand, based on how they play. As cards are revealed your odds of winning change and each player has a better idea of their position. The best Poker Players play the player across the table not just their hands. Why? Because, poker players make data driven decisions based on both deductive and inductive reasoning/observations.

During the buying process the average consumer has a very limited amount of information and or misinformation from research or misleading articles or opinions. Our job as industry experts (sales people) is to properly qualify the consumer and provide a solution for their specific situation/problem. We are selling a product or service, but closing an idea. Just like poker, there is a rule set and win conditions that are binary in nature.

The best salespeople just like the best poker players are great at talking, observing and reading 'tells'. My favorite poker player is Daniel Negreanu, because he's a talker and he is able to extract information from other players. In fact he is so good at it, that compilation videos have been made in where he guesses another player's hand so accurately that the other player folds.

Our job as salespeople is to leverage our knowledge and identify possible solutions for consumers by demonstrating value via benefits. Often we forget that the consumer doesn't know what we know. We spend all day in our environment talking to people who understand our environment. Most consumers are looking for some guidance during the buying process and some consumers know exactly what they need/want. So, whether you are new to selling or a seasoned pro, take it one step at a time.

In this book we are going to cover everything from creating a sales process to prospecting. Most importantly of all, if you find something that works for you in this book, adopt it and make it your own. I cannot stress this enough, always be closing and always be ethical. Enjoy!

"Great things in business are never done by one person. They're done by a team of people." – Steve Jobs

Chapter 1: Introduction

Why'd I write this book?

I believe selling is a learnable skillset, not some magical arbitrary process that results in one person giving the other money. Sales isn't like any other field of study, industry or occupation. It's an industry that allows any person, from any background and any level of education to be the purveyor of their own financial destiny. Why did I write this book? I believe that anyone can be taught to sell and succeed in sales. The unfortunate reality in our industry is that we do not openly share best practices. We guard them under the moniker of trade secrets. When I first started selling, a lot of my success was purely a result of me being a charismatic person. Unfortunately, charisma alone isn't a strategy for long term sales success. I wrote this book, because it took a considerable amount of research, trial & error and failing forward to figure out how to become a successful salesperson.

Why do you want to be a salesperson?

In sales, you will constantly be faced with rejection, set up meetings where nobody shows up, deal with angry customers and have doors literally shut in your face. So, before we get started let me ask you a few questions.

- Why do you want to be a salesperson?
- Why do you want to do this?
- Why would anybody want to be a salesperson?

In baseball, to be a professional you fail at your job 80% of the time and if you fail 70% of the time you're an All-star. In sales, 20% of the sales people write 80% of the business or generate 80% of all the sales. Knowing that, let me ask you some additional questions.

- Are you willing to put up with the constant rejection?
- Are you willing to go thru the struggle?
- Are you capable of handling the rejection?
- At what point are you willing to throw in the towel?
- In other words, how much failure can you tolerate?

As a reader, I want you to think long and hard about these questions before you embark on your journey. I realize that what I'm asking you to do isn't an easy task. Sales as a profession isn't for the faint of heart.

What is selling?

Selling is simply the process of one person convincing, persuading or reasoning another person to buy a good or service. A salesperson is conventionally defined by Webster as, *"A person who sells an organizations products or services to customers."* Two integral components of being a salesperson are learning how to influence and learning how to persuade. Basically, I want something that you have (money), so how do I get you to give me the money for something that I offer (stuff/service/things)?

What is Influence?

Influence is the ability for someone to convince another to take action. An influencer can be defined as, *"Individuals who have the power to affect purchase decisions of others because of their (real or perceived) authority, knowledge, position, or relationship. In consumer spending, member of a peer group or reference group act as influencers. In business to business (organizational) buying, internal employees or external consultants act as influencers."*

There are two types of influence, there is what I like to call organic & non-organic influence. The first type is influence based on genuine consent otherwise known as organic influence. The second type is influence that is non-organic and based on authority, dominance and or ascendancy. So, how do we distinguish between the two?

Organic Influence – A person's ability to persuade, convince, alter behavior of others without fear, threat and or pressure.

Non-Organic Influence – Influence based on power dynamics. For instance, your boss has tremendous amount of Non-Organic Influence over your behavior. Let's say one day your boss walks into your office and says, "Do this or you're fired!"

What is Persuasion?

Persuasion can be defined by Webster as, "To cause someone to accept a point of view or to undertake a course of action by means of argument, reasoning or entreaty."

What do you do really well?

As a reader, let me ask you a question, what do you do really well? To clarify, not what you sort of do well. What do you do really well? The truth is that most people never take the time to understand what (in life) they do really well. For instance, let's look at a sports team. On a sports team you have clearly identifiable players. A pitcher throws the ball and a catcher most of the time catches it. Knowing your position is important, but in that position what is your greatest core competency. A pitcher can have many different types of pitches, but which one is your clearly definable 'sweet spot' or 'GO-TO'? Warren Buffet describes it similarly in that, 'Every great business has a moat guarding the castle.' So, let me ask you a few more questions.

- What is your moat?
- What do you do in your role better than anyone else?
- What do other people do better than you? And how can you adopt those methods, approaches or skills?
- What unique skill have you developed to the point of absolute certainty?

Why should everyone learn to sell?

I'm going to take a controversial stance and that is, everyone in life has to sell, but not everyone in life should be a salesperson. Every day we find ourselves involved in some type of negotiation, every single day we have to sell and every job or activity in life requires some degree of sales skills. Every time your kid asks for dessert, every time you put your turn signal on to get over, every time you interview for a job, every time you ask your boss for a raise, every time you ask for discount and every time you just want something in life you have to sell it. Everything in life is negotiable, more or less. If we accept that as fact, then selling becomes quite a valuable skillset to learn. How do you get what you want in life? The easiest system I learned was to start by asking for it.

Limited Information Game

In many ways, selling is a lot like playing a game of poker. Poker is classified as a limited information game. Meaning you have to make decisions based on limited information and for every decision you make, there are implied odds of winning and losing. Although there is chance involved, as a player you have a set number of variables and some degree of certainty as to the quality of decision you are making. Poker like selling is a zero sum game, in that you either win or lose based mostly on your decisions. Instinct will only get you so far in poker and in sales, often you are going to have to rely on very limited evidence.

Different Types of Salespeople

There are three distinctive sales approaches or sales styles. There is transactional selling which focusing on efficiency measures, the more interpersonal relationship style of selling and the more nuanced approach dubbed as consultative selling.

A **Transactional** salesperson is a salesperson who focuses mostly on saving price or making price the focal point of the conversation. The focus for transactional salespeople is purely numerical and limited in scope. The conversation revolves around price, discounts and equating savings to value. What can I do for you as a salesperson? I can do is save you money on your XYZ.

A **Relationship** oriented salesperson is a salesperson who focuses mostly on building relationships. A salesperson who relies on relationship development, spends a significant amount of time understanding the customer as a person and traditional rapport building. What can I do for you as a salesperson? I can be there to care for you as a person and not a number.

A **Consultative** salesperson is a salesperson who focuses on value selling over selling on price. A consultative salesperson spends most of the time focusing on uncovering needs and discovering solutions to meet those needs. Consultative approaches often rely on open ended questions, advice and guidance. What can I do for you as a salesperson? I can educate you on your needs and help you see the larger picture.

What makes a great salesperson?

Firstly, product knowledge is key to selling. Why? Because, you need to know what you're talking about! But, product knowledge alone doesn't sell products and alone doesn't make a great salesperson. Secondly, a great salesperson needs to be a great educator, but education alone doesn't equate to great success in sales. Thirdly, a great salesperson needs to be a conversationalist, but conversations alone do not create sales. Fourthly, a great salesperson needs to be a great observer, of body language, of opportunity and an observer of people. Fifthly, a great salesperson needs to be a great detective, but merely detecting these needs will not close deals.

Opening a sale vs Closing a sale

Most modern sales books predominantly focus on the importance of the closing process. Do you know what separates a good from great? In my opinion, is a strong focus on the open and not just the close. Why? Because, the more useful information I can gather is at the beginning of the sales process. If I gather more information at the onset of the conversation I won't get ambushed with an unforeseen objection during the close. Focusing on the open allows us to build up greater consumer loyalty and 'buy-in'. The more we can understand the consumer; their wants, needs and expectations, the less buyer's remorse you can expect down the road.

Fundamentally, I believe that sales if done correctly is a front loaded process. In which we spend most of the time at the beginning of the process as opposed to the end of the process. Closing should be the easiest part of the sale, if and only if we take the time to understand the needs of the client on the frontend of the process. Let me ask you a couple of questions.

- How do you think your time is better invested?

- Asking a consumer to buy a product once?
- Or asking five different ways and undermining their reasons not to buy?

Selling can be a confrontational process it could be a collaborative process. If we do it right, closing the sale should quick and easy. Remember, in sales like in any great movie, it starts with great opening to get the audience buy-in.

Knowledge is Power

Have you ever heard the cheesy cliché, "Knowledge is power?" The hardest lesson to learn in selling is how to not talk your way out of a sale. What do I mean by that? What I mean is learning the hard lesson of when to shut up and stop talking. Remember, you are the expert and the consumer will most likely need some kind of guidance. Learn your craft and learn everything you can about the industry you choose to sell in. Learn about your products, learn about the consumers, learn about the benefits, the pitfalls and learn from the best.

Find a Mentor

What is a mentor?

According to www.oycp.com a mentor is defined as, "A mentor is a person or friend who guides a less experienced person by building trust and modeling positive behaviors. An effective mentor understands that his or her role is to be dependable, engaged, authentic, and tuned into the needs of the mentee."

How do I go about getting a mentor?

Finding a formalized mentoring process can be quite difficult. In your eagerness to learn you may want to avoid out and out asking someone to be your mentor, it's rather awkward. Remember, not everyone is an open book and or willing to help you. Start by connecting, asking for a referral and or asking questions. When connecting with someone on social media, try asking for referrals. Try something simple, such as, "Great connecting with you. It looks like we know quite a few people in common. Do you happen to know anyone in the BLANK business or who is an (Insert Occupation)."

Why should I get a mentor?

When we are too close to a business problem, we often have a hard time zooming out and looking at the bigger picture. Mentoring isn't for everyone, but finding a mentor is the easiest way to pick up a skillset, knowledge and or experience. Think of it like an occupational coach. Except this coach can help expand your network, your skills, increase your confidence and help navigate your company's culture/politics.

Mentoring Misconceptions

Writer Jeff Goins brings up 4 great points in regards to common mentoring misconceptions, *"Mentoring is about me. I need to wait for a mentor to find me. Being mentored is more passive than active. I need to ask someone to mentor me up-front."*

Embedding

Why do you think most people don't take the advice of others? Have you heard of the term **embedding**? Sometimes we latch onto the first bit of information we are offered and tend to ignore new information that may completely disprove or contradict that same first bit of information.

Author Example: Embedding

When I first started in sales, I figured out that I basically knew nothing about selling and there were people around me that I could learn from, people who knew more than nothing. So, I embarked out on a journey to find the best salespeople and tried to figure out what they did differently than me. What made them successful in sales, what kind of obstacles did they run into along the way? At first, I just merely sat back and observed my peers. My father has a simple rule about carpentry, 'Measure twice and cut once.' So, I sat back and figured out who the best salespeople were in the organization. I took parts of this person's process and that person's process. I learned dozens of tactics, tricks and tips. After a while of tactical observation I began asking questions. What I've found is that successful people love talking about what makes them successful, how they became successful and the times prior to being successful. I took all of that data, put it into a big bag and shook it up. I learned as much as I could and started adapting it to fit my process. Figure out what makes successful people successful and as my old boss always said, 'admire & acquire'.

Sell Me This 'Pen'

In the movie the *Wolf of WallStreet* there is a now infamous scene mirroring Jordan Belfort's in-person live sales training. In the scene, Jordan Belfort asks his sales training attendees to, "Sell me this Pen..." The point of the exercise is not to actually see if someone can sell a pen. The idea behind the exercise is to see how someone thinks on their feet and what their process would look like when selling a pen. It's an exercise that is meant to reveal the selling skills of the person being asked the question.

New Salesperson Example: This pen has black ink and blue ink cartridges built into it. This pen is reliable and is made of a high quality metal. I think you should really buy this pen.

More Experienced Salesperson Example:

How long have you been in the market for a pen? How often do you find yourself using a pen? What kind of pen do you currently use? Why are you looking now? What kind of activities do you find yourself doing when using a pen? Why are those activities important to you? What have your experiences been in the past using pens? When you purchase a pen what are your expectations of that pen? Describe the ideal pen? What's holding you back from buying that pen?

What's the difference between a novice and pro?

The 'new' salesperson (in the above example) is spending time focusing on talking about the features of the pen. While on the other hand the more experienced salesperson is qualifying the costumer, by asking a combination of open and closed questions. Think of it like buying a car. Most people have a preference when it comes to color, budget, on seats, cup-holder placement, the car brand, etc. People have wants, desires, needs and preferences. All of these things drive purchasing behavior and decision making when we buy stuff. If your prospect had a bad experience with a certain car, shouldn't you find that out before you try getting them into the same car?

Selling Statistics

There was this sales persistency study that was ran about twenty years ago or so. The study found that about '**<u>80% of accounts will only buy what you sell at point of sale.</u>**' To explain, ask yourself this question, "If the salesperson didn't sell me or recommend me this new product/service at the onset of the relationship, what changed?" *These are not my stats below, I don't remember where I found them otherwise I would quote the source.*

Only 2% of sales occur at the first meeting. Why do you think this is? Some customers take a considerable amount of time, diligence and patience when choosing to buy.

The closing ratio for an in person sale averages about 50%, while the closing ratio via phone/email is around 11%. I'm not sure how well this stat holds up in a Post-Corona Virus world, but when you're sitting in front of someone you can easily detect buying signals and build a better rapport. Also, over the phone it's easier to say 'no', it's easier to walk away from the sale and it's harder to build rapport.

Call back rates on messages left on leads are below 1%. This is a question I get a lot. Should I leave a voicemail message? The argument can be made that any callbacks are good investments, because if someone calls back a sales message they are probably a high intent buyer. I always found that automated message delivery systems tended dividends.

6 touchpoints are needed to convert a lead into a solid prospect. On average it takes about 6 touch points to convert a cold lead into a viable lead with intent to purchase. A touch point is merely a contact of some kind. Today's consumers are bombarded daily with thousands of advertisements and offers. Today's consumers also have access to more information than any other time in human history, which means you transparency is more important than ever.

Only 17% of all marketing emails are opened/read. This is going to vary based on industry, brand awareness and relevant relationship. Emailing is a great follow up tool, but for the most part people don't read marketing emails. When was the last time you read through and clicked through on a marketing email for a company you don't currently do business with? Odds are it was a while ago.

98% of text messages are opened/read. Texting is the most valuable marketing tool in your arsenal. Why? Because, people read their text messages.

Don't give up to easily. In sales, people will say no, people will say yes and people will say maybe.

People by our vary nature take a defensive posture when talking to sales people. The degree to that defensiveness varies from one person to the next. That being said, it's normal and should be expected for people to give you some kind of pushback. I know, how shocking, not everyone just lays down and says yes to everything that comes out of your mouth, crazy right? Did you know that according to author Robert Clay of Marketing Wizdom;

- 44% of sales people give up after one no.
- 22% give up after two no's.
- 14% give up after three no's.
- 12% give up after four no's.

The probability of reaching a contact drastically increases with an increased contact attempt. For instance, there is around a 50% chance of contact (depending on time of day) on the first call. If the salesperson makes 6 or 7 attempts on that prospect, then the chance of contact increases from 50% to 96%. Conversely, the odds of a salesperson making those calls disintegrates.

Should you leave a message when cold calling?

There is a lot of debate on this topic. If I call someone and they don't pick up, what are the odds of returning a phone call or voicemail message? How eager are you to return a phone call to a total stranger, especially when that stranger is a telemarketer? From my experience and industry research returned voicemails are almost nil.

Fictional Sales Persistency Example (Boiler Room)

Below is a fictional dialogue from my favorite sales movie 'Boiler Room'.

Seth: (Phone rings) Hello?

Ron from the Daily News: Hi, Mr. David, this is Ron from the Daily News. How you doing' this morning?

Seth: It's Davis, and I'm not interested.

Ron: Okay, I'm sorry to have bothered you. Have a nice day.

Seth: Wait a minute. Wait, that's your pitch? You consider that a sales call?

Ron: Well, um...

Seth: You know, I get a call from you guys every Saturday and it's always the same half assed attempt. If you guys want to close me, you should sell me.

Ron: All right.

Seth: All right. Start again.

Ron: Okay. Hi, this is Ron from the Daily News. How you doing' this morning?

Seth: Shitty. What do you want?

Ron: It's not what I want, sir. It's what you want.

Seth: Ron, now we're talking'. All right. What are you selling me?

Ron: I'm offering you a subscription to the Daily News at a substantially reduced price. We're trying to reach out to people that have never had home delivery before.

Seth: Right, so, basically, everybody who already has a subscription is getting ****end on this one?

Ron: Yeah, I guess so.

Seth: All right, well, I can handle that. So, tell me, why should I buy your paper? I mean, you know, why... Why shouldn't I get the Times or the Voice, you know?

Ron: Well, the Village Voice is free, sir, so if you want it, you should certainly pick it up. But the Daily News offers you something no other paper can: a real taste of New York. We have the best features, more photographs than any other daily in New York and we have the most reliable delivery in the city. Now what do you think?

Seth: You know what I think, Ron? I think that was a sales call. Good job, buddy.

Ron: So you going to buy a subscription?

Seth: No, I already get the Times.

What did you learn from this example? If you have the time I would recommend watching the scene. This is a prime example of how salespeople tend to give up too easily.

Top Five Rules of Success in Sales

1. **Have a Process.** Have a process for everything you do. If someone calls you and wants X, have a system. Have a follow up system. Have a system to cross sell. Have a system to handle objections. Just have a system.

2. **Network Every Day.** Why is today called the present? Because, life is a gift. Networking is the easiest way to build your sales practice. The more people you know the more you can leverage those connections. The more people you have in your network the more referrals you are bound to get.

3. **Follow Up**. What's the biggest mistake most salespeople make? They have no follow up game. You might be a master closer, but if you don't follow up you are leaving money on the table. When I started consulting for salespeople, after being one, the number one compliment I received was how accessible I was and how fast I was to return calls/emails. If someone calls you the least you could do is return a phone call.

4. **Don't instantly give up if someone says no.**
   When someone says no, sometimes it means no
   and sometimes it means I don't know. I don't
   know about you, I don't know about your
   company, I don't know if I actually want this. A
   no in sales can often be a stalling tactic or used
   to put comfortable thinking distance between
   the prospect and the salesperson. I'm not
   recommending that you be pushy, but learn to
   ask questions and foster a dialogue.

5. **Read about your industry for 30 minutes
   every day.** Product knowledge alone doesn't
   not produce sales success. But, the worst
   response you can give a customer is, "I don't
   know." Read about your industry and become an
   expert.

What does a Salesman do? Why do we need them?

Aren't we just another cog in the wheel? Are we necessary anymore? What value do salespeople bring to the purchasing process? The truth is sales is a crowded field, and with emerging alternative distribution channels our field will only become more competitive over time. So, why do we need people like you and me? It's simple, people need guidance, people enjoy talking to other human beings, some people are paralyzed by too much information, some people don't want to bother looking into something, some people view you as a 'CYA' and others refrain from taking action or making decisions. By in large consumers want someone to trust, still prefer a person over a computer, for now at least, and most importantly of all consumers don't know what they don't know. Look I can do all the research in the world and waste my time becoming a vacuum expert, or I can walk into Sears and ask a salesperson for a recommendation.

If sales is an **odds** game, how do I increase my odds of making a sale?

- Start by dressing professionally, even if you work from home. How you carry yourself can tell me a lot about how you value yourself. Surprisingly, a lot of salespeople dress like they just rolled out of bed. Grooming, dress and demeanor can tell you a lot about a prospect and be even more revealing abut a salesperson.

- Learn to smile when presenting and prospecting. Speech is a mixture of what we're saying, our body language and how we say something. So, if you sell over the phone make sure you smile, because believe it or not people can pick up on that.

- Take what you do seriously. Be serious about being serious. What do I mean by this? I mean you're your profession serious, act accordingly.

- Learn your strengths and your weaknesses. How often do you sit down and write down your skill sets? How often do you think about you?

- If you sell over the phone, then make **more** phone calls.

- If you sell over email, then send **more** emails.

- Don't wear a pinky ring! A lot of salespeople like to wear flashy watches or pinky rings and to me this is a deal killer. The only people I remember growing up wearing pinky rings were the Godfather and Dr. No.

- Don't be pushy. There is nothing worse in this world then a pushy salesperson... Learn to be persistent, but avoid pushy.

- Ask a lot of open ended questions. The more relevant information you can gather the better.

- Do a proper needs analysis or needs assessment. Someone doesn't walk on a lot unless they wish to purchase a car, they sure don't do it for their health! Someone doesn't call for a quote unless they plan on purchasing a plan.

Challenges Facing Modern Salespeople

What's getting in your way of closing more sales? There are an innumerable amount obstacles standing in our way as sales people. But, these are not insurmountable problems, they are just challenges we must adapt to and find ways to overcome.

- Proliferation of Information

- Advertisement Fatigue and Aloofness

- Hyper Competitive Environment

- Industry Aversion and Stigma

Consumer Advertisement Bombardment Oversaturation

According to Media Matters, "a typical adult has potential daily exposure to about 600- 625 ads in any form. 272 of these exposures come from the major traditional media (TV, radio, magazines, and newspapers)." There is an interesting social experiment going on Brazil, where one of their towns made it illegal for outdoor advertisement. Why? The theory is actually very intriguing, the theory is with less visual indication of where a business is located, we have to actually do research and talk to others.

Hyper-Competitive Price Environment

The rising tide of prices is an inevitability in sales, meaning that your product or service will increase in price, it's going to happen. When your prices go up, and they will, it's all part of the sales process and natural course of business. There will always be some underpriced competitors you will have to deal with. Price leadership is the equivalent to a race to Zero or race to the bottom. So, don't focus on price. If all you talk about is price, that is what the consumer will focus on as well. Price is a factor in all of our purchasing decisions, but it doesn't have to be the focal point. Do not fall into the price complaint pit. If your prices go up, you just got a raise! There is an old saying in sales, "Some will and some won't, but who cares because someone is always looking." If you can believe that philosophy, your career in sales will become infinitely easier.

General Expertise / Jack of All Trade Syndrome

Information historically has been hard to obtain or would take at least require a modicum of effort to get your hands on. Think about doing your homework in the 1970's. You went to the library, if the library was open, walked around to find the right book to complete the assignment, if they had the book in stock, and if you were lucky enough completed your homework. Back then it took time. Now in 2018 (2020 by the time I publish book), we have more information at our fingertips than any other generation before us. Think about that for a second. How the world has changed over time and how the proliferation of information has made your life easier. From a sales perspective, consumers are now armed with more information than they know what to do with. I brought this up because, my belief, is that as a salesperson you can no longer expect success as a general expert on every subject. Let's use insurance sales as an example, an Agent can sell over 50 types of insurance products with over 50 insurance carriers to choose from with only two licenses. How can that Agent possibly know 50 product lines in great detail? If you try to be the master of everything, eventually you will find that you have become the master of nothing.

Sales Stigma

By in large the term salesperson has somewhat of a stigma attached to it. When you think of a salesperson, what words come to mind? Pushy? Sleazy? Flashy dresser? Does thinking of talking to a salesperson produce happy thoughts or thoughts of dread? Why do you think that is? In my opinion, from working with thousands of salespeople over the years, its lack of proper training which leads salespeople to become desperate and pushy. Although we are going to talk a lot about structured sales training in this book, most companies fall short in the sales training department. What selling really comes down to is your ability to hold a conversation. Remember, someone isn't going to sit down with you unless they are interested in what you have to sell.

Sales Aversion

Have you ever talked to a salesperson who told you, "I'm not a salesman, I'm an advisor...?" If you work on commission, news flash, you are a salesperson. We do not get paid to merely educate clients, we get paid to sell. Selling as a profession is one of the most noble and non-discriminatory professions in the world. Think about it. Anyone of any background, no matter how diverse or adverse can learn to sell and become a millionaire. Someone with very little formal education can earn as much as a doctor or lawyer. Yet, for some reason it seems like people would rather run from a swarm of bees than call themselves a salesperson or get a 'sales' job. Why? Well, in my estimation it's our own fault as salespeople. Cheesy salespeople along with stale contrived bait and switch sales tactics have permeated this profession for years.

Later on in this book we're going to talk about 'owning the concept' that you sell, the first concept you have to own is the fact you are a salesperson. Why? Because, consumers and prospects can read your body language and presentation is half the battle. If you are hesitant about your actual profession or your purpose, people can instinctively pick up on the vibes you send out.

We instinctively want to follow a leader and most consumers are looking for some kind of guidance. Have you ever rode a horse? Horses are incredibly smart animals, like people, they can pick up on the rider's intelligence level. If the horse knows it's smarter than the rider, the horse takes you for a ride. If the horse senses you are smarter, you go for a ride on the horse.

Two Most Common Questions from New Salespeople

Surprisingly, most new salespeople have the same two foundational questions. Firstly, "How do I present on value?" Secondly, "How do I show a client that I care?" Price is only a factor in the absences of value being demonstrated and understood by the consumer. The simplest definition of selling comes down to seeing enough people and saying the right things to those people. If you talk about what people care about, then you can show them you care. Later on in this book we will do a deep dive into that concept and how to actually execute it.

The first step to understanding sales is understanding the absolute basics of selling, simple right? The most basic concept to grasp with sales is

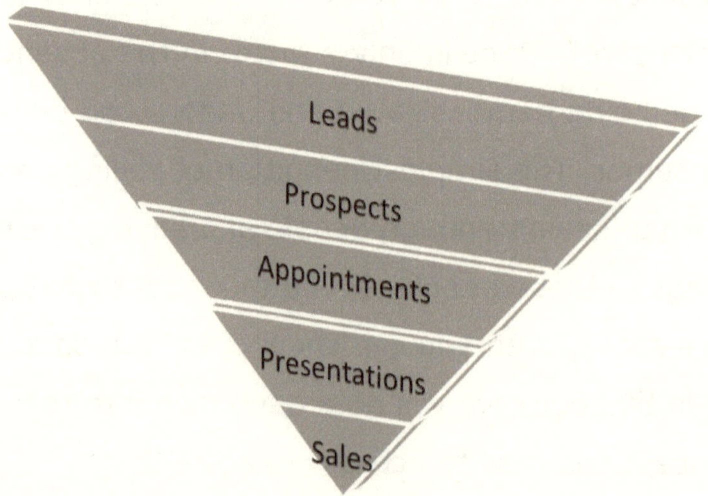

the sales funnel. The **sales funnel** is just an easy visual representation of viewing the sales process. (See below)

Leads

Leads are just names and phone numbers. Fundamentally, there are just two types of leads.

- Cold Leads
- Warm Leads

Cold Leads are phone numbers and names. **Warms leads** are known also as prospects or a lead with the intent to buy. Which at this stage in the game simply means they have some interest in giving you more information.

Lead Generation is the most taxing and laborious part of the sales funnel. Working leads is the most essential part of the sales process and generally the most overlooked, because it's the hardest. Remember, a broken clock is right at least twice a day. Even if you can't sell, you will eventually find people willing to just buy.

Also, as you begin to contact leads, it's critically important to track your progress. The leading indicator to future success for lead gen is tracking contact rate %. **Contact Rate %** tracks the number of leads you are able to get in touch with, how many people actually pick up the phone. For instance, at 9am your contact rate for cold leads might be 10% and at 5PM could be 35%. It's a simple formula, Phone Calls / Answered Calls. Knowing this information is critically important for **time-blocking** and efficiently working leads.

Prospecting

Where does the term Prospecting come from? According to my second grade history books, it comes from the actions of prospectors during the California gold rush. Think of what a prospector did. The prospector would go to a shallow river bed and sift through dirt. They would take some dirt and fill a pan with some water and swish it around. After sifting thru the dirt a prospector would attempt to find gold flakes or nuggets. The prospector wasn't trying to force the dirt into become gold, but rather spending time discovering and uncovering gold.

As we work leads and move them down the sales funnel, our job as salespeople is to gather useful information. The more pertinent information we can gather the stronger our presentation will end up being. **Prospects** are simply the leads willing to give you more information. Among your prospect list there will be prospects willing to give you time and sit for a presentation. Not all prospects will want to set time aside to hear your presentation. That being said it's important to track your Scheduled Rate %, or how many prospects agreed to an appointment. The simplest way to think about prospecting is not finding people to speak with, it's about finding qualified people to speak with or finding the right people to speak with.

The goal of prospecting is to:

- Set an Appointment with a qualified buyer.

We do this by:

- Nurturing the lead by gathering data and building rapport.

Appointments

As we progress further down the sales funnel we have our appointments. As a salesperson or sales manager one of the most useful tracking metrics you have is your Show Rate and your Confirm Rate. Your show rate is the actual percentage of people who show up to the appointment. Your Confirm rate would be the percentage of prospects that received a confirmation email, call and or message in regards to the appointment time.

Presentations

During the appointment is when you give your presentation. Again, of those meetings not all prospects will sit for the entire presentation. Some prospects will drop off during the process, it happens. Among those appointments how many presentations were given or what percentage of meetings were actually completed.

Sales

After going thru that entire process, the prospect either gives you one of three possible overarching answers. (These are not literal, they are categorical)

- Yes, I'll take it.

- No, I won't take it.

- Maybe, in which you can schedule a follow up.

After we receive one of these yes, no and or maybe's we can figure out what your closing ratio is. Your closing ratio is simply a measurement of your effectiveness as a salesperson. How many accounts were closed divided by the number of presentations given?

If the client says yes, then you have acquired a new client and convinced them to buy your product. If the prospect says no or maybe, then you can simply add or put them back into the top of the funnel and try again later.

Understanding Learning

In this part of the book we are going to dedicate some shelf space to talking about how we learn. As salespeople it's important to understand how clients receive and perceive information. It's also paramount to our own development and success that we understand how we learn. All of the textbooks in the world will not make you a great salesman. It takes practice, understanding and the ability to make adjustments. What books will do is show you a way to succeed, new ideas, different approaches and or alternative viewpoints that in the long run help you understand different ways of thinking.

4 levels of learning

In my books I like to touch on the concept of the 4 tiers of learning. Many years ago Dr. Calvin Sun expressed this simple '4 stages of learning concept' (See below). It's a simple progressive framework for looking at the developmental potential of learning.

Stage 1: Unconsciously Incompetent - I don't know what I don't know. This is the starting point for every single person who wants to learn a skill.

Stage 2: Consciously incompetent – I don't know anything, but at least I know it. This stage of learning is the awareness stage.

Stage 3: Consciously competent – You're good at something but you can't do it with your eyes closed and the task requires extreme concentration.

Stage 4: Unconsciously competent – Mastered a skill and can execute without thinking. For instance, tying your shoe laces, how many people have to actually think about how to do it?

How Long Does it Take to Master A Skill?

So, the real question is how long does it take to become unconsciously competent at a skill? The best estimate is expressed in the book "Outliers: The Story of Success" which states that, '...it takes about 10,000 hours or 5 years of full time practice to become an expert and master a skill.' This is why reading is fundamental, just because you do something for 5 years doesn't necessarily make you a subject matter expert.

The Cone of Learning

About 60 years ago a scientist named Edgar Dale developed what is referred to as the "Cone of Learning." The cone of learning effectively just demonstrates how effectively we absorb and retain information. Illustrated below by National Training Laboratories, Bethel, Maine.

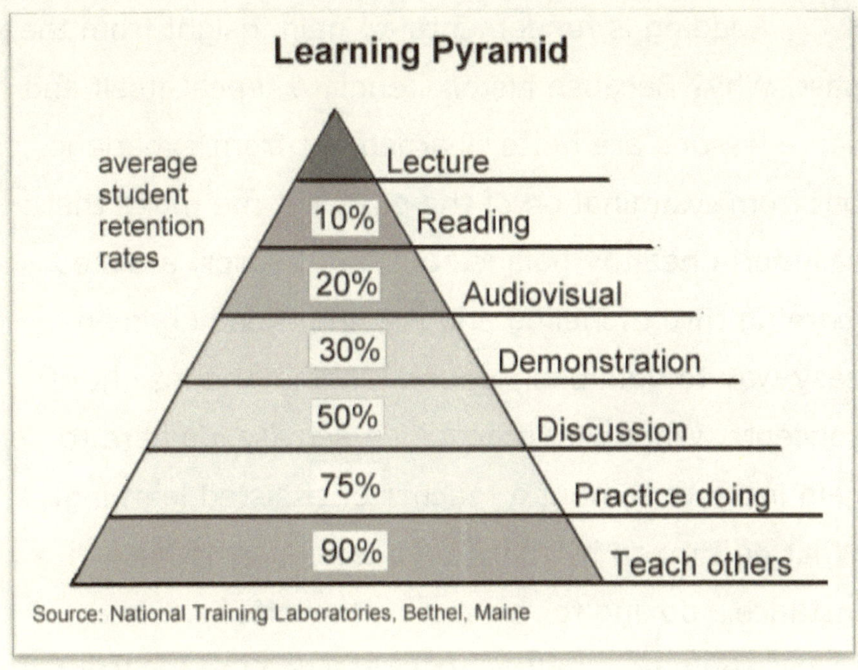

While reading this book make sure to jot down notes and underline useful information, hopefully there will be a lot of it by the time you finish reading. According to learning literature our memory recall increases, '*When we write down a statement we read (in our own verbiage) we increase the ability to retain that information by 500%.*'

Reading is fundamental to gain insight from the past. Why? Because history tends to repeat itself and some lessons are better learned not from experience, but from examination of the past. Let me make the case for a healthy balance of trial by error, assisted learning thru modeling and reading. Reading is an easy way to gain basic understanding and insight of concepts. When you practice an activity it's hard to gain insights without a teacher or assisted learning. What do I mean by that? Let's take a sport for instance... boxing for example. How effective of a boxer would you be if all you did was read books on boxing? What would happen if you stepped into the ring with... let's say Mike Tyson? You might get a hard life lesson via 'on the job training'. But, if all you do is step into the ring and try to learn by sparring, without insight or a trainer. What it takes to become competent at a skill is a combination of learning modalities, because experience alone doesn't equate to the create excellence.

Glen Gary Glen Ross as a critique on sales culture.

Alec Baldwin's character to me is the perfect embodiment of everything that is wrong with modern sales training. Sales training is not about motivating salespeople through shaming and or belittling. Effective sales training is based around learning new systems and process mastery. Where do most sales training programs go wrong? In my opinion, they focus too much, even exclusively on the 'What' of sales and not the 'Why' and 'How'. For instance, anyone can master a product or learn product features and furthermore any salesman can be a walking talking product guide, but that doesn't mean you can sell. Motivation is telling us why to do something, but not how to do something. Sales training should be 10% motivation or belief building and 90% process improvement.

Alec Baldwin's character spends the entire opening dialogue of the movie with a sales training speech. A speech that in no short order completely demoralizes the people he is trying to train. The title of the training should have been, "I can do this, why can't you???" One of his most infamous lines in the speech is, 'I can go out tonight with the leads you got and make myself $50,000.' Well, that's great that **you** can do that. It's self-evident **you** can do that, otherwise you wouldn't be training people. Most salesforces are so competitive they guard sales processes like some massive trade secret.

If you are a sales trainer or sales manager, don't focus only on goals, focus on building a culture of educational collaboration and role playing. Goals are meaningless without skills. I think too many sales managers focus on goals and not driving behaviors that feed into the goals. Think of it like building a muscle, it doesn't happen after one rep. Sometimes it takes hundreds if not thousands of reps to build a muscle. Simply identifying a problem and categorizing a problem doesn't fix the problem. It merely identifies there is a problem. Imagine going to a doctor and the doctor saying, "Hey your back is broken, why can't your back not be broken like mine?" You know your back is broken, that's why you came to the doctor, for a solution. I know this seems self-evident, but most sales managers can't help fix your back, they merely tell you its broken.

"There are two great days in a person's life - the day we are born and the day we discover why." –William Barclay

Chapter 2: Networking & Prospecting

Networking versus Prospecting

For the purposes of being specific Networking is defined as, *"The process of developing and using your contacts to increase your business, enhance your knowledge, expand your sphere of influence or serve your community."* Whereas Prospecting can be defined as, *"The search for potential customers or buyers."*

What is the Goal of Networking?

The goal of a networker is to build their network. When networking you are looking for referral sources, potential clients and or anyone who can act as a conduit to your success. Networking is really that simple.

What is the Goal of Prospecting?

Prospecting is the process of simply nurturing leads until they can commit to a scheduled appointment. The goal of prospecting pure and simple is to identify qualified leads and convincing those leads to set appointments.

What prospecting is and is not.

Prospecting is not turning a lead into an appointment for the sake of an appointment. Prospecting involves qualifying a lead and gathering information. Why? Because, unqualified prospects should not buy your product and most likely are going to waste your time. For instance, think of a 'prospector' in the traditional sense of the word. Think of the gold rush and how a prospector found gold. A prospector is filtering and sifting out dirt to find gold flakes. A prospector is not trying to turn the dirt into gold.

First Impressions and Prospecting/Networking

You have exactly 7 seconds to make a good first impression. So, what's your plan? What are you going to say to be different? How am I going to know that I can trust you? Why should someone give you the 8th second?

What is the biggest challenge for most people who want to learn how to network? The problem or challenge most people face is rooted in fear. Fear of what? Fear of being rejected? No, it's the same fear of public speaking that most people have. Animals have three reactions to danger; flight, fight and freeze.

What is the problem most people have when networking? The problem most people have is that they are simply unsure of how to be interesting or afraid of not being interested. I think of it like insurance, the law of large numbers. The more people you speak with the better your odds. What I hear a lot of new sales people say, "Mike, I don't want to be the guy at the event standing in the corner... alone."

But, Mike how do I be interesting?

If you want to learn how to be interesting then first you need to learn how to be interested. Asking questions is the best way to break the ice. Well, what do people care about? People care about their stuff, ideas, concepts, themselves and their family. What I've found is that most people tend to have the same favorite subject... themselves. There is no better explanation of networking then, "All things being equal people will do business with, and refer business to, those people they know, like, and trust." – Bob Burg

Would it help you to know what people talk about? Would it help you to know why people talk about what they talk about? People tend to talk about the same 4 subjects of conversation:

- **People**

- **Things**

- **Ideas / Concepts**

- **Events**

"Great minds discuss ideas; average minds discuss events; small minds discuss people." – Eleanor Roosevelt

Don't overthink it. Some people like to talk about others, some people like to talk about what they read in the newspaper, some people like to talk about concepts or ideas. Some people like to talk about current events, or past events.

We tend to associate with people who talk about similar subjects. People who talk about other people tend to find friends who like talking a lot about other people. People who talk about concepts and ideas tend to have deep interesting what-if conversations. For me, when I meet someone, I like to know what they like to know. What do they do? What interests this person? Why do they do what they do? Do they enjoy what they do? What do they enjoy about their vocation or occupation? Do they like sports?

Example: Using Tesla

People – People are easy to talk about. For instance, Elon Musk is constantly in the news and constantly changing the world.

Ideas – What do you think America will look like in 50 years? When do you think self-driving cars will take over the car market? What do you think about self-driving cars? Why do you think only 10% of Americans have a retirement plan?

Events – Did you hear about the Self-Driving car in Arizona that ran over a pedestrian? Events are a great way to stir up conversation.

Things – Self Driving Tesla Model 3. That is a physical and tangible thing.

Rapport Building Processes

- What do you do for a living? Or how did you get involved in this activity?

- How long have you been doing it for?

- How do you like it? What do you like about it?

- What do you do really well?

Other Rapport Prospecting Questions

- With your Company, tell me about the people who built it. Tell me about the people who are building it.

- How old is your company/charity?

- Where has your company been? (History)

- Where is your company at now?

- Where is it going? (Vision)

- How's life?

- Tell me about yourself.

Find out what a person is reading.

What are you reading lately? This is one of my go to questions for networking, because I've found that most successful people tend to read. I once came across a statistic that stated, 'If you read 1 book per month in your given field of study, that in less than 5 years you will be among the top 5% of subject matter experts in that field of study.'

Rapport Building

When I train salespeople I make a simple ask. I ask them to bring something from their cubicle. I'll ask for two things in particular. One is a prospect sheet they're working on. The second and more important is something unique from their desk. I'll take the quote sheet and start asking a series of qualifying questions.

- What does the client care about?
- How can I tell from this quote sheet?
- How do you know?

- What are they concerned about?
- Why are they buying?
- Why are they buying from you?
- Why are they buying now?

Then I'll take the object from the desk and start asking the person about it.

- Why do you have this on your desk? Well, it's a picture of my family.
- It sounds like BLANK is really important to you, can I ask why?

The answer is obvious, but my point is sometimes we don't ask the prospect 'what they put on their desk'. People put things on their desk that remind them of things they care about.

Remember, people talk a lot about things they care about. Start with some basic questions to stir the conversation.

- Does this person have a family?
- Do they have kids?
- Who is in the household?
- What is their vocation?
- What is their career?
- How long have they been doing that for?
- Why did they start in that role?

- How did that become to be?

- What do you do for fun? Do you volunteer?

- What do you do in your down time?

- When you're not out buying a new car or
  quoting your insurance or buying vitamins, what
  do you do for fun?

- What do you like about all of that?

- Why did you get involved?

- Why do you keep doing it?

- What keeps you going?

Remember, most people love to talk about themselves. It's everyone's favorite subject, until they have kids. So, get them talking.

Clearing Out a Room

Do you know the best way to walk away from a social networking group with no connections? Go into a lengthy diatribe about the numerous benefits of your product/service and how amazing you are. When opening or when networking, ask yourself this question, "When I leave here how will people describe me?" As the obnoxious insurance agent who couldn't stop talking about himself, or possibly as someone who is transforming an industry by putting a focus on protecting middle class families?

Networking, if done correctly, focuses on leading with your ability to communicate benefits. How can I help this person? Most people tend to think of networking as, 'what can they get from that person'. Regardless of how you want to build a network, try to lead with questions that uncover a need. When being approached or solicited most people operate on a simple litmus test, what's in it for me? What does this person know that I do not? More importantly, why does it matter?

Unique Value Proposition – UVP

How do you explain to people what you do? Better yet, how do you want to be remembered? How will others describe what you do? What is your differentiator? Warren Buffet says that, 'Any great business needs a moat to survive and protect the castle (business).' Or a very specific differentiator that the competition doesn't have access to yet. This comes back to what you do really well. In any sales profession, there will be ups and downs. Sometimes you will have the luxury of the lowest most competitive price or product and other times you will have to play defense. Why should a consumer buy from you and not the guy down the street? Because, you have a nice smile? Because, they like doing business with you? Or do you offer something of value?

Developing Your Unique Value Proposition

What do you do? Who do you want to serve? How do you do what you do it? Why do you do what you do? What's in it for that other person? For example, "I help families, due X by doing Y." Can someone easily decipher what you do and how you do it? Does it play with your marketplace? Is it down to earth or 'Pie in the Sky'? Will it stick in my head when you say it? Can I trust you? Is it dependable, verifiable and credible? What is your theme? Is it positive and upbeat? Why does it matter to me?

Follow Up On Social Media

Social Media is the business card of the future. When someone asks you for a business card, I normally respond by asking if they have a social media account. Social Media can be a great way for efficient follow up systems. What do most people do with business cards? They throw them away or lose them.

Example of Follow Up: "Hey John, it was great meeting you at XYZ event. It looks like you're doing great things in your industry."

Follow up Insight: Depending on the person you are networking with you can share articles on their blog or share videos they have made. Instead of just liking and sharing what a person posts, try to add some insight or thoughtfully respond.

Example of E-Follow Up: "Hi John, it looks like know some people in common (if true). It was great meeting you at X networking event and learning how you are transforming the BLANK industry. INSERT YOUR ASK HERE."

Note from Author

The scripts in this book are very generic on purpose. The point of the script examples found in this book are for you to develop and begin to craft your scripts and processes. The scripts are broad and will provide some guidance as you create your own. The point is not to provide a comprehensive script that works in every situation.

Don't Overthink Networking

Networking is a simple process that merely involves talking to enough people and saying the right things. Not everyone you meet will click with you. It's a numbers game, pure and simple. Don't try to be the star of the show and don't sit in a corner. Actively work the room and meet people. Ask for introductions and build relationships.

Networking is not a competition.

Although networking is a numbers game, you need to get quality contacts. So, spend the right amount of time with each person. Set a goal for what you want out of the networking event. You don't just want to be the revolving door of the event. Every networking event I attend my goal is simple. I want to walk away with two really good contacts before I leave the event.

Networking Buddies – Dynamic Duo

If you're uncomfortable solo networking, then try to bring a buddy. Groups tend to grow exponentially and people tend to gravitate towards groups of other people. Every networking event I go to I make it a point to bring someone. Having a buddy can really help you avoid some of the awkward moments of trying to break the ice and meet new people.

Throw Out a Line

Don't think people are out of your league or below your pay grade. Network with everyone all the time. When I do networking training classes I get this question, "Would you network with people below your current pay band, etc., etc.?" My answer is always a resounding yes. Why? Because, where you never know who might end up being your boss one day.

Incidental Similarities

Incidental similarities are the core elements of rapport building methodologies. Researchers at the University of British Columbia conducted a study on, "The Persuasive role of Incidental Similarity on Attitudes and Purchase Intentions in a Sales Context." This study showed that, 'Incidental similarities between the buyer and seller and significantly increase the buying experience of the customer.' For example, in application Disney Theme Parks emblazoned their employee names tags with the hometowns of the employee. What the study found was that guest and employee experiences increased as people from similar towns interacted. How as a sales manager can you exploit this potential opportunity? Jonathan Becher of SAP points out that, "… in a group of 23 people, the chance two people have the same birthday is greater than 50%!" As a salesperson this follows the Bob Burg rule that, 'People tend to do business with those they know, like and trust.'

Networking Mistakes

Networking is more of a science than people give it credit for. When I started networking it was somewhat of a foreign language to me. As I read about techniques and tips it allowed me to make small adjustments to my process. That being said, networking is not an exact science and different strategies can work for different salespeople. As far as common mistakes and missteps most experts can agree on the following.

- Having unrealistic expectations ahead of an event.

- Not playing the numbers, talking to too few people.

- Not following up, lack of follow-thru.

- Having an approach that is too casual for the event

- Lack of specificity

- Lack of patience, in regards to results.

- Too much talking about yourself, not others.

- Showing up unprepared, preparation is key.

Unrealistic Expectations Going Into an Event.

When setting goals and expectations for networking, try to avoid setting too lofty of goals. What I mean is that networking is a marathon not a sprint. It's an incremental game that involves a lot of contact and a lot of follow up. Don't expect to get before you give and by osmosis every single person you meet will feel obligated to send you business.

Not Playing the Numbers

Networking is all about talking to enough people and saying the right things. Even if you don't know how to say the right things you can still stumble into a sale if you play the numbers. Sales is a contact sport, the more people you contact the better the odds of winning.

Not Following Up

Most salespeople lack scheduled and planned follow up. When you meet someone and want to foster a business relationship, don't forget to plan a follow up. When you follow up it shows you care. People tend to spend time on things we care about. Thusly, even small overtures show a lot of value and consideration. Dedicate some time each day to following up and don't be afraid to throw out multiple follow up emails/calls. The most effective way to network is asking for a follow up at the event for a future date, get some buy-in. For example, "Hey John, it was great meeting you at XYZ networking event last week. Your approach on BLANK could be a huge asset to my clients. Would you be able to hammer out some time in your schedule this week to talk?"

A Too Casual Approach

Sometimes we forget to be our professional selves and we drop our guard. When I meet people at networking events I always shake hands. I don't fist bump, I don't go in for a hug and I don't act like I do around my friends. Avoid using personal emails accounts, especially if your email is not professional. For instance, one my first emails was **itchybo@email.com**. Which was a nickname given to me by Mike Scioscia at a baseball camp in the early 90's. Stick to a professional email address, even if it's a personal email service.

Lack of Specificity

Knowing what to say is half the battle with networking. When we connect with other business professionals we need to be clear with our intentions and clear with our messaging. For instance, why should this CPA refer you clients? Not only why, but which clients should the CPA refer? What do you do and why should I care? What is your ask?

Patience is a Virtue

Don't expect massive results from day one. Relationships our fostered over time and require opportunity to organically grow. This concept comes back to setting expectations and caring. If you want to find referral partners or key people within organizations to network with, be patient. Remember those wise words from the greatest movie ever made, Field of Dreams, "If you build it they will come."

Talking too much About You

An easy mistake most nervous sales people make is not knowing when to stop talking. Sales is a game of asking questions and leveraging the answers to demonstrate value. You have two ears and one mouth, act accordingly. <u>Don't talk exclusively about yourself</u>. No one cares how much you know until they know how much you care. Just have a conversation and see where it goes. Can you hold a conversation? Do you know when to let your foot off the gas? Do you know when to pump the gas? Do you know when to do a 180?

Showing Up Unprepared

Preparation is a leading indicator of your success in sales and the same goes for marketing. Find out who is going to the networking meeting in advance, when possible. Practice your elevator pitch and don't wing it.

Author Example: Preparation

One of my colleagues once told me, "It doesn't pay to be an expert." A little context, he was going to a life insurance and group benefits sales call that required in my mind a lot of preparation and knowledge to execute. When I asked him if he was an expert on the subject, he said, "All you have to do is read about (the subject) the night before the sales call and that way you're more of an expert than the prospect." It was almost an unbelievable conversation. You can probably guess the outcome of that sales call, it rhymes with disastrous.

Properly Dealing with Gatekeepers

What is a gatekeeper? A **gatekeeper** is the person in charge of communicating or preventing communication from reaching the decision maker. For instance, a gatekeeper could be a secretary or receptionist or assistant of said decision maker. So, now we know what a gatekeeper is, how do we get to the decision maker?

Here are the two most common strategies to get past your typical Gatekeepers:

1. Leave the information with the Gatekeeper.

2. Convince the Gatekeeper to get an appointment with the decision maker.

What is the ultimate goal of prospecting? To set appointments with the decision maker. Which of the two above strategies is easier to execute? The first strategy is far easier to execute, but tends to not produce the desired result of setting an appointment with the decision maker. What happens when you leave information with a gatekeeper? Think about it from the perspective of a gatekeeper. The gatekeeper is generally extremely busy and probably sees 10 to 20 salespeople a week asking for business and or dropping off leaflets. Getting past gatekeepers will take practice and persistency, there is no one size fits all approach.

Finding the Decision Maker

After we have successfully bypassed the gatekeeper now we have to determine who the decision maker is. A **decision maker** is simply someone who can make a decision. In partnerships or multiple owner businesses you have a single decision maker or multiple decision makers who can be responsible for purchases and contracting. Remember, as salespeople our ultimate goal is to make sales, we cannot do this without being able to talk to the right people. So, make sure to find out if the person you set up an appointment with has the authority to even make a final decision.

"Every great dream begins with a dreamer. Always remember, you have within you the strength, the patience, and the passion to reach for the stars to change the world." Harriet Tubman

Chapter 3: Understanding Consumer Psychology and Buying Behavior

Chapter 3: Understating Consumer Psychology and Buying Behavior

In this chapter we are going to discuss the most important part of the buying process, the consumer. Because, without the customer we don't make a sale. We're going to discuss why people buy, when people buy, what people are thinking when they buy and most important of all how to understand it all. If you don't have the money right now to take an MBA level Marketing-Psychology course then I'll save you some money, 'People hate to be sold, but love to buy things.'

Types of Consumers

Some consumers care about having a brand name and some could care less. Some consumers are price driven and some are less price sensitive. Some consumers value relationships and some do not. Some consumers trust no-one to get the job done, so they classify themselves as Do-it-yourselfers. Some consumers are shopping around because all they care about is finding a new company to be with, I call these consumers Vengeance shoppers. Maybe the consumer had a bad experience with billing, salespeople, financing, reliability, customer service, after hour's service, paperwork and or any other thing that could go wrong. Some consumers buy to support charity or causes they support. Some consumers prefer being educated and guided thru a process and would pay a little more for that. Some consumers only care about making their life easier. Some consumers only want to buy face to face and some over the phone or via the web.

When I train salespeople I like to ask a broad question, 'what do clients care about?' Roughly speaking, about 90% of salespeople give me the same answer. What do you figure that is? Most people chime in with price as the answer. To which I say, why do people buy this product? Is price the root cause of a purchase decision? Most of the time it's not. Price is the cost of value. Price is merely a cost for a product or service. Price for the most part is only an objection when the client is not qualified to purchase the product/service and there is no underlying need/want to be fulfilled. As a salesperson it's important not to steer the conversation towards price. Talk about price, it's part of all of our buying decisions.

Have you flushed out their belief systems?

Belief systems are defined by Webster as, "a set of principles or tenets which together form the basis of a religion, philosophy, or moral code." Consumers for the most part are different and unique. Who knows how to spend their money better, you're client or you? The answer is obvious, you're client. Don't spend the client's money for them. Don't presume to know what people believe or care about.

For example, when I was an insurance agent I would want to know rather quickly how the person felt about insurance. Why? Because, there are two types of belief systems with insurance. The first is that insurance is a maintenance policy and used for every possible claim no matter the size of the claim. The second type of consumer is the consumer who believes that insurance is for the big stuff, for the catastrophic losses.

Framing a Question

There is an important effect in behavioral science called the 'framing effect', which states that when proposed a question in a different way people will act differently in their response. Which means that how we ask questions is more important than what we are asking.

Feel vs Think people

There are two types of people in this world. There are feel people and then there are think people. Some people are emotional thinkers and some people are analytical thinkers. How can we tell the difference? Typically people will self-identify depending how they respond to questions. For example a person could say that, "I really think that... or I really feel that..." Why is this important? Feel people tend to respond to stories, anecdotes and parables. While Think people tend to respond to numbers, facts and stats. If you pitch numbers to a feel person you might completely lose them. If you start to tell prior customer stories to a think person you might miss the mark.

A simple example.

Have you ever listened to a debate and thought, "That one debater is just making sense to me and that other debater doesn't make sense to me at all." Or have you ever wondered why people in a debate rarely ever persuade one another? This happens all the time on social media platforms, two people get into a ruckus political discussion that results in everyone losing their cool. Why do you think that is? Because, people don't bother to listen and understand the communication preference of the other person. When we don't know the preferred communication style of the other person we often just talk at them and not talk with them.

How do we talk to feel people?

Feel People:
Campfire Stories, Parables and Antidotes.

How do we talk to think people?

Think People:
Numbers, Facts and Figures.

How do you identify feel people?

Feel Person: Tell me more about that… I really feel that… Or I felt that… I just don't feel that I need…

How do you identify think people?

Think Person: I really think that… I thought that… I'm not thinking about that for another…

Why do People buy things?

Why do people buy things? Consumers buy things for many different reasons. For instance, maybe the consumer is purchasing a home for the first time or buying an investment property for the first time. Maybe the consumer is no longer a fan of their bank because their bank was setting up fraudulent auto insurance policies without consent. Maybe the consumer is shopping because they want a lower price or maybe they want a better **bargain**. As we discuss consumer segmentation next, remember people are individuals, but as groups we tend to make very predictable and similar decisions.

Understanding Consumer Segmentation

Effectively you can break down consumer segmentation into four main classifications. They are as follows:

1. Geographic Segmentation

2. Demographic Segmentation

3. Behavioral Segmentation

4. Psychographic Segmentation

1. Geographical

Proximal distance between customers. For example, customers who live within 25 miles of the business or customers who live outside of 25 miles of the business. Other geographical categories are rural consumers or metropolitan consumers.

2. Demographic

Age, Gender, Occupation, economic status, income, religion, etc.

3. Behavioral

Impulse buyers, people who wait until the last minute, early adopters, etc.

4. Psychographic

Customers who are vegan, customers who buy organic, customers who shop based on brand loyalty, customers who only buy trucks, etc.

Why should we Segment?

The better we understand consumers helps us customer our approach for each consumer. For instance, in my practice I would pick up clients at the golf course. Why? Because, I love to golf and when you golf you have captive audience for nearly 3 hours. Everything comes back to increasing your implied odds. How can we increase your odds at selling an account? Segmentation models can increase your odds. For example, if your insurance company provides a 15% discount to accountants, would it benefit you to market to accountants?

Consumer Life Stages

Why should we understand consumer life stages? Would it benefit you to know that your product has a 50% close ratio with Young Singles and a 1% close ratio with Newlyweds? Would it benefit you to know that 90% of clients written last month were New Parents? Plain and simple, if we can determine where we 'play' best, we can be more effective salespeople. Here are some but not all consumer life stages:

- Single
- Young Couples without Children
- Married/Single without children
- Married/Single with Children
- Married/Single children in College
- Empty Nestor
- Retired
- New Entrant,
- Young Singles,
- Young Couples,
- Couples with Children,
- Newlyweds,
- New Parent,
- Single Parent,

- Empty Nestor,
- Divorced/Separated/Widowed,
- Pre-Retiree and Mature/Retired,
- Blended families and Sandwiched families.

Super Normal Stimuli

Why do we want to own big shiny things? Why is gold worth more than silver? Even though silver has a much higher practical industrial use? Or even before silver had a higher practical industrial purpose, 2000 years ago, why was gold more intrinsically more valuable than silver? Why do people buy things outside of their budget? Why do people want the biggest and the best? Why do we keep up with the joneses? The answer... Perception is reality and it's genetically coded into our DNA.

Don't take my word for it. Nobel Prize winning scientist Nikolaas Tinbergen noted in a study:

'Nikolaas constructed plaster eggs to see which a bird preferred to sit on, finding that they would select those that were larger, had more defined markings, or more saturated color—a dayglow-bright one with black polka dots would be selected over the bird's own pale, dappled eggs.'

Space invaders

Do you ever think about how close is too close to someone? What I mean is do we ever think about how far away we should stand to people in a social setting? When you meet someone for the first time how close is too close and how far away is too far away? What's the objective measure for distance and personal space? Judging space is tough. As a rule of thumb the personal space radius of comfortability is about 3 feet or so.

Space Invader Exercise

When I run meetings on how to network, I often do this simple exercise. All you have to do is have someone stand up and have them come over and shake your hand. But, then as they come towards you take a big step in their direction and see their reaction. Most people clam up or stop in their boots.

Why do I need an online presence?

There are three reasons why you need to have an online presence; consumers have a greater ease of access to information, prices are hyper competitive and brand reputation. Remember, just because you don't look at your website or social media, doesn't mean prospects will not.

Access to Information: Let's be honest consumers have access to 90 to 100% of the information available to make an informed buying decision about your product or service. But, how many consumers do the proper research online or have the time to do the proper research? Probably, very few. More and more consumers are relying on the internet for information, because, in part, they've had bad experiences with salespeople. In my industry 75% of consumers now go online for quotes and information before contacting a company, broker or agent. Which to me is great. A lot of agents look at this as a challenge, but it's really a great opportunity in disguise. Information can be confusing, ambiguous and hard to decipher, which means as an expert you can add value.

Price Environment: The price environment for most salespeople is hyper competitive. Products and services are being driven down in price, due to the internet and people forgetting how to sell on value. Selling on price in my opinion is a race to zero and doesn't require a lot of sales skill.

Reputation: Your brand reputation needs to be built, maintained and defended online. Many companies make the mistake of not doing this and think the internet is still a fad. People are looking at your website, even if you are not. This is part and parcel due to the change in societal referral mechanisms, along with the proliferation of information online. What I mean is that people used to spend a lot of time talking to their neighbors and now they look at on-line reviews or the posts of their online neighbors. Most people who go online to review do so because they have a bad experience and not a good experience.

Here are the facts according to H. Lewis
Yildirimturk of Reputationbuilder.us:

- 88 percent of people trust online reviews as much as they trust their best friends' recommendations.

- 80 percent of people choose to go elsewhere if they read bad reviews of your business online.

- Customers who have a bad experience are twice to three times more likely to write an angry review than customers who had a great experience are to post a happy review.

- One negative review online (when not countered by positive reviews) can cost up to 30 new customers.

- It takes 12 positive reviews to cancel out the nasty side effects of just one negative review.

Why Consumers Appreciate Customization

People are unique and different. Which means that people appreciate feeling that they have been treated as an individual and not just another notch on your sales board. When you're able to tailor your approach and customize the offering it will add a tremendous amount goodwill during the sales process. Goodwill can be defined as, "friendly, helpful, or cooperative feelings or attitude."

Author Example

I learned this lesson the hard way. When I was signing up a client for an insurance policy I stumbled into the 'payment ask'. This was a client that I had previously had and my rapport was strong. So my blunder was this, "Most of my clients pay on a monthly basis..." To which the client responded, "I don't care what most of your clients do, I pay quarterly, all that matters is how I want to pay." Now granted I took advantage of the level of rapport in this situation, but it was an invaluable learning lesson. People want customization based on their needs not the general public.

"There are two great days in a person's life - the day we are born and the day we discover why." – Eleanor Roosevelt

Chapter 4: Mental Game of a Salesman

Chapter 4: Mental Game of a Salesman

Mentality of a Salesman

In this chapter we are going to discuss what many experts call the, 'Inner Game of Sales.' Selling is not an exact science and process you can control, some of it's an art form. That being said, often a much overlooked aspect of selling is your state of mind. So, we are going to talk about ways to deal with sales aversion, overcome your internalized objections and approach selling with fortitude.

External Activities to Increase Sales Skills

Here is the first activity I want you to try. When you try to purchase a product or a service ask for a discount. You'd be surprised how much money you can save. Does that seem reasonable? Heck no it doesn't, but once you start doing it often enough, it becomes second nature and then becomes reasonable over time. Last week, I went to Jersey Mikes with my buddy, I didn't order anything, but I took a water out of the fridge as it was 100 degrees outside. When I got to the check-out I asked, "Hey, I didn't order anything do you mind if I have this water bottle?" Surprisingly, I got a free water bottle that day.

The second thing you should try is simply taking a different route home from work. We tend to get stuck into out predictable routines. How often do you take a separate route home from work? Odds are you have a consistent route and it feels uncomfortable to break your habit.

Focus on what you can control.

Every time something happens ask yourself, 'Is this within my span of control?' Is it internal or external? Do I have the ability to control this? You cannot control a bad economy nor can we control whether people choose to buy or not. You can control how many phone calls you make per day. You can control how many emails you send. You can control how many books you read. You can control how many networking events you go to. You can control how many salespeople you learn from. You can control how many follow up meetings you set. You can control how often you call other salespeople to secret shop the competition.

Your mind is your most powerful tool or your most powerful distraction. I can't tell you how often I see people on a car lot sitting around talking to each other. Last time I checked, although it might be mentally stimulant, it won't produce sales to chit-chat with co-workers and shoot the breeze. It's important as you pursue a career in selling that you understand and realize that your mind needs to be re-focused like a camera lense once you lose sight of the target. Think of your mind kind of like an attic, everything you learn in life causes a synapse to fold and imprints on your memory and is stored in that attic. Like any attic there is a limited quantity of space. So, it's extremely important to make sure you put valuable information in that attic, that way it doesn't get cluttered with non-valuable information.

Control your language.

Later on in this book we will discuss the power of self-affirming statements. The focus for this part of the book will be on your own internal voice. For instance, saying that, "I'm broke or don't have any money." How much good do you think that does to your psyche? Not much in my estimation. If you read self-help books or sales books, they often just tell you to, 'think positive and your problems magically disappear.' In this book however, we are going to focus on solution based thinking or a solution based mindset. It's easy to identify that your bank account is low on funds, but how do you plan on fixing it? Why not try, "How do/can I make more money?" You can sit around all day and say, "I need to make more money, I need to make more money, and I need to make more money." At the end of the day it comes down to habits, your process and your follow up.

What motivates you?

Why do you do what you do? Recognition? Money? Ego? Why are you doing this? There are many easier career paths you could be embarking on. Why sales? What makes it worth it for you? Why do you stay in the game? My grandfather used to tell me a story about his buddy Ralph, back in the day they used to be door-to-door life salesmen. One day, he was door knocking and looked over at Ralph's clip board. On his clipboard was pinner a picture of his family. He used it as a constant reminder as to why he was doing what he did.

tutto finisce

"Everything comes to an end." When I network, sell and or work I do so with this statement in mind. Why? Because, it's the truth. Every business fails eventually. Every job comes to an end. This is the kind of mentality that will help you get over rejection. Because, what do you have to lose? If you knew your job had a countdown clock, how would you act differently? When you are constantly in fear of losing your job, you act a lot differently then knowing it comes to an end no matter what you do.

Time Management is everything.

Do you ever wonder why some of your co-workers constantly stress out or find it hard to meet deadlines? Or why some people seem to always be working around the clock only before an important deadline? At the same time, do you have co-workers who consistently finish on time or ahead of schedule? Both people share something in common, time management.

Time is by far the most important commodity in your life. We cannot buy more of it, we cannot buy it back and we have a finite amount. Worst of all we have no idea how much we have left. Time management is one of the most important skills you can ever learn. Time can be your best friend or your worst enemy. How you manage that time will determine a lot about the quality of your work life. So, here are a few tactics to help you develop your time management skills.

Be authentic

Don't run away or shy away from who you are as a person. Instead why not just own it? Being inauthentic or insincere can be damaging to your reputation and ability to just get along with other people. Why lie or omit from others? For me I always found it easiest to be open and honest, that way at least you know where other people stand in life. I'm the guy who shows up early to everything, which drives some people nuts, but that's me.

Time as an Investment

According to a recent study, it found that the average person spends about 2 hours per day browsing social media. Along with that, the average American watches about 5 hours of television per day! So, that means the average person is going to spend 20% of their life either watching TV or surfing the web. You will be spending 20% of your life or 31% of your awake day wasting time. Even worse yet you'll be spending about 40 to 50% of your awake non-working time staring on a phone or tablet.

Every salesperson manages time differently. That being said, here are four ways to think differently about your time management:

1. Time blocking

2. Schedule your calendar

3. Send Confirmations

4. Write down a daily to-do list

Firstly, time block.

Time-blocking is hard for most people to grasp. Time blocking is important, because we tend to get lost in our work sometimes and need to remember to prioritize. Schedule and reserve certain parts of your day for certain activities and tasks. You'll find that certain hours will have more reliable show times and call back times. Schedule time for daily preparation. Don't let your schedule control you, control your schedule.

Secondly, Learn to Schedule your Calendar out.

If I don't have my calendar with me, I'm somewhat useless these days. My calendar is my memory. Learn to schedule out your calendar as far in advance as you can. Staying organized is not easy, but it's worth it.

Third, find time to confirm.

When you time block find time to confirm your appointments ahead of time. Show rates for most sales appointments are rather low. People have lives to live and things come up, life happens. A **show-rate** is just the percentage of appointments kept. For instance, you schedule 10 appointments and 5 people show up for the scheduled appointments which means you have a 50% show rate.

Author Example

We once had one our insurance brokers drive over two hours for an unconfirmed appointment. The prospect never showed up or bothered calling the broker to let him know that he wasn't going to show up for the appointment. So, naturally after talking to the broker I asked a simple question, "Did you confirm the appointment?" Now granted that wasn't the question he wanted to hear, but never let a bad situation go to good waste. Needless to say that was the last time he did not confirm an appointment.

Lastly, write down your to-do list.

Each and every day, I take a pad of paper out and write down my to-do list. That way I can prioritize my tasks for the day and easily stay on task. Keep all of your tasks top of mind by writing them down and checking them off one by one.

Why do most Salespeople fail?

- They don't stick to a process.

- They don't ask questions.

- They don't know when to ask questions.

- They talk too much about them.

- They do not listen enough.

- They don't read books.

- They don't know their product inside and out.

- Don't forget to take breaks throughout your day. Remember, this job can be incredibly taxing, make sure to take some you time. My rule of thumb is that for every hour of work we should walk for 5 minutes.

The Power of Self-affirmation

Self-affirmations are thoughts or behaviors that support and or strengthen our perceived integrity of our 'self'. For me growing up watching boxing, time and time again Muhammed Ali would always shout, "I am the greatest." In a study ran by Schmeichel & Vohs 2009, showed that participants who engaged in self-affirmations were able to significantly change the way they thought about tasks and goals.

How you choose talk about yourself is how people will perceive you. I'm not saying to walk around telling strangers you are the greatest salesman in the history of salespeople. What I'm saying is that before you can be successful you need to think that you can be successful. You need to believe success is possible.

Commitment

When the Vikings sailed to a new land they would burn the ships so they had no choice but to keep moving forward. I'm not saying that you should have a backup plan in life. I'm saying you need to obsess over being successful in sales. When people talk too much about having a backup plan I always think that, you're planning to fail before you even plan to succeed. Why not fail forward? Why fall backwards? When I say fail forward, go all in. Play your hand all the way. Don't be the person who starts a bunch of new things and never finishes.

"Quality is not an act it's a habit." –Aristotle

Chapter 5: Cross Selling and Upselling

Chapter 5: Cross Selling and Up-Selling

In this chapter we are going to discuss the importance of cross-selling and up-selling. We're going to look at how to cross-sell, how to up-sell, why to cross-sell and why to upsell or if upselling makes sense for your business.

Cross Selling

Cross Selling: Cross selling is a sales strategy to persuade the consumer to buy multiple related products/services to compliment the underlying purchase.

> For example, a personal trainer who sells his/her service can sell supplements alongside providing training to complement the underlying service provided.

> For instance, an auto insurance broker or agent can offer multiple lines of related insurance, such as, Umbrella Insurance or Life Insurance.

Up Selling

Up Selling: Up Selling is the strategy based on increasing the price of a sale by adding on additional features or purchasing a larger quantity and or purchasing a better product/service.

> For example, let's say a consumer wants to purchase 10 training sessions from you, but you convince them to purchase 15 to get a better price per session.
>
> For instance, a car salesman can sell a car, but up sell a customer on nicer features, such as, GPS, etc., etc.

An example I often use when training salespeople is talking about my first insurance shopping experience, post being an agent myself. I sent out some requests to local agencies. There was a single agency that dominated the SEO rankings and predominantly featured on the search engine. Naturally this was my first choice. I sent a very-very specific request of what I was looking for; an auto, renters and umbrella policy. At the time I was renting, so to another agent that might not seem like the most attractive client. I made a rather simple request and received back an email with bare bones coverages, no attempt to cross-sell, no attempt to up-sell, no attempt to meet in person, no attempt to build rapport, etc. Either way, my point is don't leave money on the table and don't spend the clients' money for them. Don't assume what a prospect qualifies for, find out with a proper needs analysis.

Up-selling: Waitress Example

According to USnews.com the average yearly earnings for a waitress in the United States is around $25,280. Let's assume that the average cost to eat out is $12.75 per meal in the United States, at least according to thesipledollar.com. If we assume that a waitress earns around 15% of $12.75, which is around $2, then we can safely say that the average waitress is serving about 50 people per day, more or less.

How can we increase your earnings as a waitperson? Three options, ask for a raise, see more customers per hour (aka work harder) and or increase the amount of money per customer (aka work smarter). Let' choose to maximize each sale, because ultimately we have some level of control over that approach. How can we maximize the sale? Well, let's start with upselling. The average "Prime Rib Cut' of steak is around $43 per meal. So, if you offer something to that extent, the easiest way to increase your income would be by throwing out a higher priced item on the menu.

If you were to ask 100% of those 50 customers per day for a Prime Rib Cut, and only 10% agreed or 5 people per day. How would that effect your overall yearly earnings? With a meager 10% close ratio on a high value entrée at your restaurant it would increase your earning potential by up to $1,516 a year! A 10% close ratio doesn't make you a master closer or master salesperson, but it will make you more money. This is a concept called the aggregation of marginal adjustments. Remember, to be a great salesperson you must first start to be great at just being consistent in your ability to ask for the sale.

Amazon Cross Selling System

Do you ever use Amazon? Talk about a company that is mastering the science of cross selling. Others who have purchased, "Introduction to the Science and Art of Selling" by Michael Bonilla have also purchased, "How to Sell Life Insurance." According to Amazon's CEO Jeff Bezos about 35% of sales on Amazon come from cross selling. As part of your process make cross selling a key element. Every time you go to Mcdonalds they ask you a simple cross selling question, "Would you like fries with that?" Why? Because it works!

Don't Spend the Clients Money for Them

How much money is someone willing to spend on your product/service? As much as they are willing to spend. I know this seems like an obvious answer, because it is. Often we view the world in our own lens. Let's say you make $50,000 a year. You live in a world of $50,000. Your purchases reflect that income, habits and behaviors. As salespeople when we view a client, we should not assume what a person is willing to pay or can afford. We need to find out by asking questions.

Up-Selling/Cross-Selling: Don't spend the client's money for them.

In early 2017 I was working with a salesperson who was quoting an Auto Insurance Policy. I asked this salesperson to tell me about the client. The client was going thru a divorce, so they were quoted minimum insurance limits per state law. I asked, why. The response I received was shocking. She said, "Well they are going thru a divorce and money is tight right now…" I asked, "How do you know what they can and cannot afford?" She said, "What do you mean?" To which I said, "Well, what I mean is that if you don't present a proposal then how can you possibly know what's important to the person and what they would be willing to purchase? Without asking?" So, your upselling system is not to ask unless your intuition notifies you that the client wants something? What I was getting to is that she made up the persons mind for them. I asked a few more questions to dig, "Why didn't you quote a renters policy, as he is now divorced and will be renting? What about an umbrella policy considering he is a business owner. She said, "Well Mike, he just wants a simple auto quote." To which I always say, "What do you have to lose by presenting on a needs basis and throwing in an umbrella and renters quote as well?" Who is the expert? Who knows how insurance works well? We started talking more and more and what the root cause of the problem was the salesperson was overworked with service tasks and didn't want to do the extra work to upsell the account. She invented an excuse to justify her strategy.

What Percentage of your prospects do you try to cross sell?

Sheldon Snodgrass, 'estimates that only about 7% of overall prospects are asked to be cross sold.' Out of 100 inquiries your salesforce is only asking around 7 to 10 percent of customer and prospects for additional products and services. Follow the money. If Amazon is driving 35% of its overall revenue from cross selling, don't you think you should look into setting up cross selling systems? How are you tracking your **Cross Sell ask rate**? Otherwise how do you know how often your team or you for that matter is asking for the cross sell opportunity?

What can Upselling do for my Income?

Here's an easy mathematical example. Let's say you make 10 sales per week for $1000 each sale and you get paid on that $1000 in commission for selling $10,000 in product. Now let's say you ask those same ten prospects to buy an add-on or higher level of "X" for an additional $150 per prospect. Let's say 5 out of 10 take you up on that additional $150 add-on. Over the next year after starting to upsell that would earn that salesperson an extra $3900 in income or 7 to 9% increase in income for just asking a question. My number one question when training salespeople is, "Why wouldn't you?"

"Great works are not performed by strength but perseverance." – Samuel Johnson

Chapter 6: Objections

Chapter 6: Objections

In this chapter we are going to discuss objections. We're going to clarify why people object, when people object, what an objection looks like, how to determine the root cause of an objection, how to handle objections and how to pre-empt objections. Objection handling is a normal part of the sales process, and should not be looked as a negative experience. Let me ask you a question, whose fault is it when a client objects? It's not a trick question, it's your fault. Objections are going to happen.

We're going to cover in some detail the following topics:

- Why people object.

- When people object.

- How to handle objections.

- What type of objections you might encounter.

- How to anticipate possible objections.

What is an objection?

Webster defines an objection as an expression or feeling of disapproval or opposition; a reason for disagreeing. For the purposes of this book, an objection is when someone indirectly or directly says no.

Why do prospects talk to salespeople?

As we discuss objections, I want you to remember that there is a reason people talk to salespeople. Prospects talk to salespeople because they have a problem (unmet want or need) and they think or feel that the salesperson has the solution.

In behavioral science there is a term called the 'Orienting Reflex', which is 'is an organism's immediate response to a change in its environment, when that change is not sudden enough to elicit the startle reflex.' This shows the importance of properly addressing questions, concerns and the prospects understanding of your sales pitch.

Tension Threshold Principle

The TTP is a simple illustration of a sales conversation. Think of the process like an EKG machine. As you go through the sales process the idea is to keep the prospect from having 'peaks and valleys'. In the diagram below, there are two key aspects of the sale that we need to keep in mind. The first is the uncertainty caused by having to wonky or brainy type of conversation, which confuses the customer. This is called the 'intellectual' threshold, which basically means you confused the person or intimidated them with knowledge. When you throw too many numbers, facts or figures at a person, there is a good chance they might object. The second threshold is the emotional, which is at the bottom of the chart. The emotional threshold is simply where you get the prospect angry, down or depressed during the conversation. If you unknowingly challenge someone's beliefs, they might object. When either one of these thresholds is crossed, the prospect will object. What I want you to take away from this principle is the fact that you control the process and are prospects will object depending on how you lead them down your process.

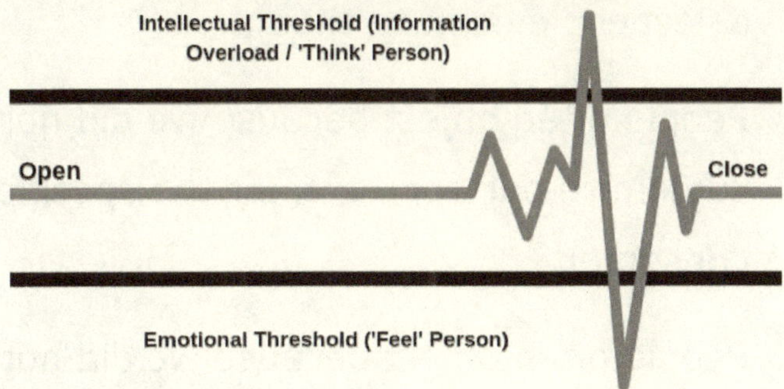

Four Components of Objection Handling

There are four core components of objection handling. They are as follows:

1. Understanding Why People Object.

2. Understanding Common Objections Consumers Use.

3. Understanding how to Pre-empt and flush out Objections.

4. Have a Process for Handling Objections.

Why do people object?

There are countless reasons why people object during the buying process. For example;

- People often object because we as salespeople confuse them.

- People often object because we did not customize our approach for the specific consumer.

- People often object because we did not address a question, need, worry, concern and or concept.

- People object because we did not find a way to help them.

- People object because we didn't show them the benefit, what is in it for them?

Underlying uncertainty

Is the prospect certain that you know what you're talking about? This comes back to the idea of trust. Is the prospect certain that your company is the company that is going to help them meet their goals/objectives? Is the prospect certain that the product or service is best suited for their needs and is consistent with their objectives.

How to categorize objections.

There are basically three or four primary categories of objections. Most people will naturally object 3 or 4 times during a sales process, if you as the salesman are asking questions and making the conversation engaging. The worst case scenario for me in the sales process was always for the prospect to not really say anything. I'm not there to spew information but to have an exchange of ideas and thoughts.

These are the four categories of objections:

1. No Time

2. No Money

3. No Need

4. No Trust

No Time

Time is the most valuable commodities we have. Some people don't want their time wasted and some people when you can are running out the door. For example, "I really don't have time right now."

No Money

Some people think your product might be too expensive of possibly cannot afford it. For instance, "I cannot afford that." Or, "That is too expensive."

No Need

Throughout this textbook we are going to talk a lot about needs and qualifying. Fundamentally, as salespeople we should not be selling products or services to prospects who are unqualified to purchase. For instance, "I'm not sure if I need that much X." Or, "I don't know if that is the right product for me."

No Trust

Trust is the one factor of a relationship that takes a long time to build and once lost is almost impossible to rebuild. To some degree trust is imbedded in all objections. For example, "I don't know you." Or, "I really don't think that company is right for me... I heard or read bad reviews or my neighbor said X about that company."

Identifying a Complaint and Identifying an Objection

Sometimes people just like to complain, it happens. All prices for all goods and services go up, it's called inflation. Think about it from the perspective of the consumer. When the price of gas goes up, how often are you jumping for joy? So then what is the difference between a straight up complaint or an objection? If an existing customer says, "My price went up!" Or they say, "That's way higher than what I paid in the 90's for that!" Is that a complaint or is that an objection? Will that lead to the customer shopping and switching providers? It depends on the customer and depends on how we approach the overall conversation.

How to determine the root cause of an objection?

What's the fastest way from point A to point B? A straight line. So, why not just ask the client? For example, "That's really interesting John, why do you say that?" Or, John, that's interesting, can you tell me more?" The sentiment that I want to present to a client is always, 'Please, tell me more...' Why? Simple, I want to get them talking, which in turn will get them thinking. Here are three good reasons why to approach an objection this way; it gives me time to understand their perspective, have a dialogue and gives me room to think about a counter point or response.

Flush Objections Out at the Onset

When is the worst time to get an objection? At the end, middle or beginning of your presentation? Would you rather deal with objections before or after they come up? How do you feel when a client drops a big old objection right after your sales pitch? What makes your life easier, hoping they do not object or flushing out objections before your close?

Understanding Common Objections Consumers Use

I don't know you! I really don't have time right now. I don't have the money. I cannot afford that. I need to talk to my wife about this. I don't think it's for me. I'm not sure. This is too expensive. I don't want to get locked into a long term agreement or contract. I'm currently stuck in a contract with my current company. I'm happy with who I'm currently with. We're downsizing right now. I've never heard of you or your company. It's really not something I want to do, it's not that important. I'm unsure what it could do for me or if it is the right fit for me. We are happy with the way we have things set up. I don't want to go thru the hassle. That product isn't compatible with how we are set up/systems. I'm just not interested. Can you call me back next year? I'm busy at the moment. I'd like to go with your company, but we cannot budget it. I read a bad review about that company. A lot of people are complaining online about that company. I DON'T KNOW YOU!

By Objecting, what is a Client telling me?

An objection, is usually, but not always a result of a mistake we make during the sales process. A prospect doesn't either understand what we are trying to say, they are confused about a concept and or the prospect is seeking more clarity.

Price as an Objection

Price is always a factor when we make buying decisions, I'd be crazy to say otherwise. If a client doesn't see value, then what do they see? They see price. Price can be a minor factor or it can be a major factor. If the salesperson is leading with price, price now has become a major factor in the buying decision. If we focus on value selling then price, for a qualified buyer, is not the predominant decision when making a purchase. A simple lesson we all need to learn is when and how to get out of our own way. Here are some tips on how to do that as a salesperson.

    a. Don't lose control of the conversation

    b. Always be the first to Agree.

    c. Speak in a tone that suggests your reasonableness.

    d. Speaking in future tense

e. Is a want or need motivating the buying decision?

Price is a surface level objection

Price, by in-large, is a surface level objection for most consumers. Price in simple terms is merely the cost of value. Why is 'Price' a surface level objection? I often ask salespeople a simple question. What do clients care about? What do consumers care about? The response I get is too often, "Price." Or something to the effect that, "People only want the cheapest thing possible."

Let me ask you something, do you want the cheapest airbag in your car? Do you want the cheapest heart surgeon operating on your child? Do you want the cheapest wood holding up your house? Do you want a car with the cheapest tires? What about a house? Do you want the cheapest possible home to live in? People are great at rationalizing things, we do it all the time. Ultimately, when the average person makes a purchasing decision, we place value above all else.

The Allen Effect

Did you know some people enjoy speaking to salespeople? What I mean is that some people are never actually interested or qualified in buying your service, yet for some reason they still want to talk to you. I call this the 'Allen' effect. One day I was cold calling, and came across a prospect named 'Allen'. I dialed and smiled for 5 hours straight and finally connected with someone interested in talking with me. We talked for about 45 minutes, and I hung up to work on his proposal. Little did I realize he had absolutely ZERO intention on buying. I used his phone number as a training tool in my brokerage. Allen was eager to give just enough information to complete a quote, and always willing to have a 'quick' sales conversation with just about anyone who called him.

The Allen effect is a great example of intention. What's the person's intention when speaking with a salesperson? To quote one of my favorite movies, "A guy doesn't walk onto the lot, lest he wants to buy a car." - Alec Baldwin, Glen Gary Glen Ross. Remember, some people can be qualified prospects and don't have no intention to buy.

Shopping Around

Let me ask you a question, what do you do when a client threatens to shop around? What I used to tell clients is the blunted truth...

Client: 'I want to shop around and see my options.'

Salesperson: 'frankly it might be the right thing for them to do.'

Salesperson: 'It sounds like getting the best possible deal is important to you and you might feel there is a better deal out there.'

Client: 'That's correct.'

Salesperson: 'Let's be honest we probably don't or will not have the absolute lowest price on the market.'

Salesperson: 'When we signed you up X years ago, why did you go with this plan?'

Client: 'At the time it was the right option for us or Insert something here.'

Salesperson: 'Do you feel that our price fair? Yes, absolutely. If there someone who can offer less than us? Possibly. But, how much time will you have to spend to find out?'

'Closability' index

Every client has a different level of agreeableness and different level of 'Closability'. For instance, some clients we consider 'lay-downs', meaning they don't object and agree with everything you say during a sales presentation. **See diagram below.** Some clients on the opposite end of the spectrum are harder to close and tend to object, and object often. Your typical prospect will object up to 4 times during a presentation and the most would be around 6 objections. Of course this will vary by industry, but for the most part you will find this to be true in sales.

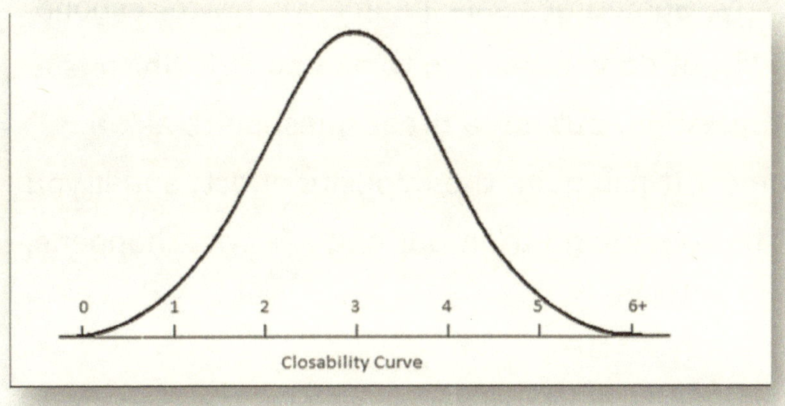

Objections are a sign of uncertainty.

Most objections are a cause of an unaddressed concern, question or some part of our process that the client is confused about. But, there's good news! The good news is that you can control most of those variables. Most prospects will have objections and an experienced salesperson should know how to leverage those objections. Objections are a good sign that the client is actually listening and engaged. The worst objection for me is, "I'll think about it." So, what are you telling me? You weren't thinking for the last hour??? That's the whole point of a conversation. Which conversely means that I didn't do my job correctly. Sometimes salespeople will try to respond with, "What do you have to think about?" Which is a great question, but not a great question to ask a customer. It has quite the opposite effect, and if you don't believe me go try it out and see what happens.

Understanding how to Pre-empt and flush out Objections.

How easy would a sales conversation be if you could just flush out the objections prior to the presentation? So, how can we do that? At this point in the book we know why and how people are going object. Selling is chess not checkers. If we can guess what someone is going to say, we can prepare our rebuttal in advance. If we are blindsided by the objection, it makes our process far more challenging that it has to be.

There are generally three objection handling strategies. They are as follows:

1. **Anticipatory**: Determine Objection Timing (Anticipate) when in the process is this objection potentially used? Once we determine the timing of an object, we can determine when and how to craft your message.

2. **Pre-empt and Flush Out**: How can we flush out the objection early in the process to handle it so it doesn't come back up later in the process and block the close? This is called Pre-empting.

3. **Sporadically Direct Handling**: Handle as they come and do no prep work. This is how most untrained salespeople deal with objections. Direct objection handling usually involves re-directing the consumer rather than actually adding value and perfecting your process. Think of this strategy as, "I'll figure it out as I go."

When a client says, "I'm need to speak to my spouse." That normally comes up either in the very beginning of the process or at the very end, but rarely does it come up in the middle. When a prospect says, "Let me think about." That normally shows up at the end of the process and not during the lead gen process or qualifying process. Either way, the first two strategies assume objections as a normal part of a sales conversation and will allow you to prepare for objections instead of trying to fight the process. A sales conversation can be collaborative or confrontational. As a takeaway here, I do believe there are direct objection handling techniques that are valid in certain doses. The third strategy is more of a checkers mentality and the first two are chess.

Example # 1: I need to talk to my spouse...

Have you ever heard a prospect say, "I think...? I should talk to my spouse, before I make this decision?" This is a fair point, because if you care about your spouse, you get them involved in decision making.

Anticipatory: This objection normally comes at the end of your process. So, knowing that how can we get ahead of this one? What can you do to prep for this objection? Think about it.

Flush Out: Why get ambushed by this objection? Why not ask in advance? Ask who makes the decision, in a subtle way, or ask who you like to consult with when making these kind of decisions?

Pre-rebuttal: Is there anyone else that we would have to consult to make this decision or are you the final decision maker? Re-word that as needed, my point is you need to ask.

Sporadically: 'Bob, is it fair to say that your spouse might have some questions about the proposal? Considering, I won't be there to explain the proposal in detail, the way I explained it to you, what kind of questions do you think she might have? Do you think she'd have questions about the Product, My Company or myself?'

Example #2: I don't have the time right now...

Most salespeople will agree this is the most common objection used by consumers. Why? Because, time is our most valuable commodity. People might feel their time is being wasted, people might have prior appointment and or commitments in place. Either way, how do we handle this?

Anticipatory: This objection can come when prospecting or working cold leads. This objection can come when trying to nurture a lead and set an appointment. This objection can come during the appointment. This is by far the most common during cold calls for consumers to get you off the phone.

Pre-Empt: Flush it out. When would you have a good ten to twenty minutes to sit down and talk about BLANK? Is this a bad time to talk? How much time do you have right now? Do you have any appointments after this? I just want to be respectful of your time, do you have any obligations after this?

There are two methodologies that lead to this objection and they are polar opposite strategies.

Search for Yes: Is this a good time to talk?

Search for No: Is this a bad time to talk?

Sporadically: Direct handling often results in the salesperson trying to rush through a presentation and or desperately trying to cling on to the conversation. There are many ways to handle this objection and later on in this book we will look at some process ways to handle it. Don't cheapen what you do by trying to condense it down based on the schedule of the other person.

Example #3: "I've read some bad reviews (online) about that company."

This is becoming a much more common objection across all industries, and there are some easy ways to handle it. Let's be real, if you look hard enough online you can find bad reviews for fresh air, puppies and rainbows.

Anticipate: When does this objection come up during the sales process? Mostly at the onset of the conversation or the discovery call.

Pre-empt: Why are you looking to switch providers? Have you done any research so far? What have you found? Do you have any preference for BLANK? Focus on asking questions around consumer experience.

Sporadically: When do people tend to leave reviews online? When they are happy or upset? Focus on the truth, and the truth is that people go online to write negative reviews. Trust me, I've gotten enough on the grammar of my books.

Have a Process for Handling Objections.

Having a consistent objection handling strategy is the key to selling and navigating the sale. Objections can pop up at anytime during the sales process and it's paramount that you develop your rebuttals. What is the difference between a confrontation and a negotiation? A key concept to any contract known as 'Agreement'. If you to attempt to shut the client down, instead of hearing them out you will put up barriers. For example, if a prospect says, "Wow, that's really expensive." Most salespeople will instinctually and incorrectly say, "Well, we can look at other options... or let me see if I can adjust... or you don't have to purchase all..." You get the idea, they instantly lose their confidence and start back tracking on the offer.

There are two common types of presentation strategies. The first is the one solution sale, having one customized offer. The second having a three choice option, three scaling choices where you want the customer to select the middle of the road choice. Generally speaking, if you go with the single choice option, when I make an offer it's because it is the right solution for the problem. In the single choice strategy, back tracking is often going to completely ruin the sale. Later on in the book we'll go a bit deeper into presentation strategies.

One objection strategy is to simply validate and move forward with the sale. For instance, "That's really expensive!" To which, I acknowledge that fact. For instance, "You're right, how would you like to pay?" I'm not here to argue with the customer, I'm here to sell the customer. This comes back to a simple question. What is your job as a salesperson during the negotiation process or the close? It's not to argue with the prospect, if you start to argue, you've already lost. Selling is not a combative process, it's a process of filtering out no-intent buyers, finding qualified buyers and closing deals. When you affirm an objection most people have the same reaction, they are confused. Why do prospects get confused? Because, most salespeople are pressure style sales people who rely too much on rebuttals and not enough on asking questions.

Complaints vs Objections

It's important that we are able to identify when people are griping and when people are objecting. Sometimes people just like to complain, it happens. If a client says, "My rates have gone up! This is unacceptable!" After hearing something like that what is your first inclination? Is it to immediately start making excuses? When you know a client is going to pay more money for something than expected, you have one of two choices. You can deal with it before it happens, be preemptive or you can do nothing and hope it goes away. If you choose the latter, then more often than not you are going to have to play a lot of defensive. Either way, this might just be a complaint and not an objection. Remember, nobody enjoys paying more for stuff. No one is going to celebrate the fact that they had a rate increase.

"Luck is great, but most of life is hard work."- Lain Duncan Smith

Chapter 7: Soft Skills

Chapter 7: Soft Skills

In this chapter we will be discussing soft skills. We'll talk about what soft skills are, which soft skills are highly desirable, how to develop soft skills and why soft skills matter.

What are soft skills?

Soft skills are defined by Webster as, "personal attributes that enable someone to interact effectively and harmoniously with other people." From one salesperson to another, your soft skills will make or break your success in sales. Some skills we'll look at in this chapter are;

- Observation

- Relative Disassociation

- Caring

- Charisma

- Dispute Resolution

- Conversationalist-ism

The foundation of any good sales is at its heart a great conversation. Sales will by in-large rely mostly on your ability to hold a conversation. Not your ability to monopolize or to dominate a conversation, but your ability to hold a conversation. Salespeople have to have the desire at all times to want to talk to other people.

Strategic Pausing

Think about the tensest scene from your favorite movie. Is there an abundance of silence or an abundance of noise? Nine times out of ten, the scene will have an abundance of an eerily fine-tuned violin with long dramatic pausing in the dialogue. Pausing is a great way to create tension and put the client in driver seat. It's a tool we can use to empower consumers to actually sit back and think and then arrive at a decision. Pausing is awkward and by its very nature prompts the other party to speak. What pausing does more than anything else, it lets the other party know that you are in control of the conversation, but willing to not monopolize the conversation. Most new salespeople get so afraid when a pause happens in the conversation they tend to just blurt out every word that pops into their brain.

Does this actually work? Yes, silence produces tension and the need for someone to respond to break the silence. Ask a question, shut up and wait for an answer. Ask for the close, shut up and wait for an answer. The first person to speak in a negotiation, often will lose that negotiation.

Matching and Mirroring

Matching and Mirroring is a simple back and forth process to help determine the relative level of client rapport. For instance, if you're sitting down across the table from a client and the client has their arms wrapped/crossed around their chest, what does that tell you about their attitude? It could mean absolutely nothing, or it could mean the client is putting up a 'guard' or it could mean the client is chilly. Regardless, 'Matching and Mirroring' is our ability to subjectively assess the comfortability of a client. For example, if a client has crossed arms, try 'M&M' by crossing your arms and see what kind of response you get. Does the client react? Do they adjust? Do they change their tune? If you're new to selling, this could all sound rather silly, but trust me it works. If a client adopts a defensive posture, what does your posture look like at the same time? If a client leans in, what do you do? If a client leans back, what do you do?

Learn to Smile

There is a study that shows when I can put you in a good mood your functional intelligence goes up by around 7 to 14 IQ points. So, learn to smile. If you want a more tangible example, think of Dwayne Johnson, Barrack Obama, Denzel Washington, and or anyone with charisma. What is the commonality that binds them together? They all smile, often.

Desirable Soft Skills for Salespeople

Soft skill development can make or break a salesperson. More derisible skill sets for sales people are; Dispute Resolution, Charisma, Negotiation, Interpersonal Skills, Deductive Reasoning, Empathy, Patience and Active Listening.

Charisma

Charisma is defined by Psychology Today as the ability to attract, charm, and influence the people around you. How do you teach charisma?

Dispute Resolution

Dealing with an angry or upset customer is not easy, but doesn't have to be difficult. People can get very frustrated dealing with salespeople, it happens. I'm a huge believer at some point in life, every single person in the world should work at a restaurant. Why? Because, people are never angrier than when they are angry and hungry at the same time. More so, working in a restaurant will help develop your sales skills. Our job is not to convince the person we are right and they are wrong, that is the easiest way to lose a sale. Our job is to collaborate and discover a need while elegantly uncovering a solution (our product/service). When you have an upset customer or prospect in front of you try this:

- Smile

- Agree that you are here to help.

- Listen

- Reaffirm what the person is saying.

Ask yourself:

- Can I fix this problem?

- How can I fix this problem?

- Who can fix this problem?

- What is the customer asking for?

- Is what the customer asking for possible?

- How can I make it possible?

Don't play the blame game and try to prove the customer wrong. Figure out how to fix the problem and move on. Although the customer is never wrong, they are not always right.

Actively Listening

Most new salespeople are so eager to present they forget to ask questions, but they also forget to listen. There was a rep that I was training who had an angry customer call and complain about price. The customer called in and talked with their neighbor, who was paying about ½ for home insurance. The client was new to the firm and had left their old firm because of poor communication with the Agent. Price was a complaint not a deal killer for this client, but with proper listening and positioning there is a simple way to remedy that situation.

What's the difference between hearing and listening? Listening is a proactive process and hearing is reactional in nature. Hearing something doesn't require skill or actual work, it requires ears. Listening requires ears, and also the thing in between those ears... your brain. Active listening involves picking up on what people are laying down and absorbing information.

The Art of Showmanship

Presentation skills and showmanship are key to your success as a salesperson. When working with new or struggling salespeople, I want to find out if they are doing group sales presentations. Why? Because, public speaking tells me a lot about a salesperson. The easiest way to start building your confidence is one step at a time, learning is a marathon not a sprint. Figure out your strengths and develop them. To develop a skill takes time, like building a muscle. If it's public speaking, develop it. If it's persuasion, pacing, tone, diction, generating excitement, etc.... develop yourself.

Reading a Client (Non-Verbal Cues)

Non-Verbal cues are the most valuable 'tells' or insight into what a person is thinking. For instance, a tell can be as simple as a person playing with their ring, strokes a pen, raises an eyebrow, coughs, etc.

Developing Sales and Soft Skills

- Take an alternate route home on your daily commute.

- Try something new at your favorite restaurant.

- Play this game with your coworkers, anytime you hear a co-worker say 'no' put a dollar into a jar. No is the killer of a sale. Choose your words carefully and selectively.

- Tell a non-linear story, tell a story with the ending first.

- Learn to remember someone's name by saying it 3 times in your head. When I run group trainings, one of the ways I get the group engaged is the fact no matter how large the group, I can call out people in the audience by name.

- Read industry material for 30 minutes day.

- Role-Play every single day or when you have free time.

- Walk and Talk. In ancient times the romans and the Greeks would walk and talk. They would walk around and philosophize together. Many ancient Greek buildings were designed around this concept.

Empathy

Psychology today defines empathy as, "Empathy is the experience of understanding another person's thoughts, feelings, and condition from their point of view, rather than from your own. You try to imagine yourself in their place in order to understand what they are feeling or experiencing. "

Tonality

The common belief among psychological research is that 55% of communication is body language, 38% is the tone of voice, and 7% are the actual words spoken during a conversation.

"There is no great genius without a touch of madness." –Aristotle

Chapter 8: Goals

Chapter 8: Goals

In this chapter we are going to discuss corporate Americas favorite overused buzzword… goals. We're going to discuss why goals are important, mistakes people make when setting goals, how to set goals, when to set goals, why goals matter and creative ways to reinforce goals.

Do you ever wonder why most people never reach their goals? Did you know that most research shows that up to 70% of projects fail to meet their stated goals? We fail to achieve goals because growth requires getting out of our comfort zone. How many people do you think follow through with their new year's resolution goals? About 80% of people fail by February. Goals should be incremental and progress in a linear fashion. Most people set big lofty goals and expect exponential growth towards that goal, that's just not how life works.

People tend to set big lofty goals. That's great, but it's better to be realistic. For instance, you make $50,000 a year now and want to set goal of making $100,000 a year by next year. Is that realistic? Let's say historically you earn a 5% raise each year. If you stay the course that means you are probably going to make around $5300 next year. So, setting a one year goal of $100,000 seems a bit unrealistic.

As we discuss goal setting in this chapter, it's important we make a simple distinction between goals and vision.

- **Goals**: the object of a person's ambition or effort; an aim or desired result.
- **Vision**: a vivid mental image of what you want your business to be at some point in the future, based on your goals and aspirations.

Two Types of Goals

There are two types of goals that are important to drive results. The first type of goal is an activity goal and the second is a result goal. Results are driven by behavior and activities. Remember sales is a numbers game and we need to play the numbers.

- **Activity Goal:** Number of phone calls to be made per day, number of follow ups, number of emails, number of networking events or groups to attend, number of people you need to see per day. How many books have you read in the past two months? These goals drive your sales results. As a sales manager it's easy to spend time crunching numbers and setting lofty goals, but ultimately just find ways to drive the activity. Activity breeds production and without prospects in the pipeline sales will not magically appear.

- **Result (sales) Goal:** These are the traditional sales goals. How much business do you want to write this month? How many widgets do you want to sell this month? How many clients do you want to sign up this month?

Stretch Goals and Incrementalism

One of my first sales jobs was as a personal trainer. It was how I paid my way through college and attending a private college gave me a lot of motivation to sell. That being said, a good personal trainer can motivate someone to be consistent and reach their goals, but a great personal trainer can push someone to achieve what they never thought possible. A great trainer can help a client see the vision, it's a little something called leadership.

To set a stretch goal, the trick is to set them just above what you think is possible. When you physically stretch, your aim is to stretch a little bit further each time you try. The mistake most people make when setting goals is that they confuse a vision with a goal. Which leads the person to setting goals laughably high or obtuse. Some people set these massive goals. So massive they tend to lose any meaning or importance.

Incrementalism is not the preferred goal setting method for most sales experts. But, as we achieve small goals we build our confidence. Incrementalism reinforces your confidence and helps you progress as your development progresses. As we achieve these small goals we become more competent and prove our own competence, which in turn will build your confidence.

Goals Incremental and Vision Monumental

Why do most people not achieve goals? Because, they confuse goals with vision. Goals should be stepping stones and a vision should be an ideal. For instance, if you don't know how to ride a bike, should your goal be to win a triathlon by Monday? Or should your goal be to learn how to ride a bike? The vision should be massive and monumental, while the goals leading to the vision should be incremental, like competing in a triathlon and winning.

How to set S.M.A.R.T goals?

What are SMART goals? The SMART goal system is a framework for establishing goals.

Specific

Let's get specific. What are you trying to achieve? Why? I want to have a $100,000 income by my 30th birthday. Why? Because, that kind of income will provide me the lifestyle I want.

Measurable

How can we measure our results? Is this goal measureable? Can you measure motivation? Can you measure inspiration? Can you measure attitude? Maybe, but sometimes we cannot quantify feelings very consistently. For instance, I want to be in good shape. That isn't an objectively measurable goal.

Attainable

Are these goals probable or possible? Are these goals within my power? Can I reach these goals? How realistic is this goal? Is this goal generic or based on your ability? Often, corporations set unrealistic goals based on 'sales math' or pick goals based on theoretical 'pie in the sky' type of thinking. For example, having a goal that I grow to 6'11 is not attainable.

Relevant

Make goals matter. Whenever a corporation sets out new goals without a why, no one tends to care about the how. Smartergoalsneverfail.com recommends you start here: "Why is this goal important to you? What are the benefits and rewards of accomplishing this goal? Why will you be able to stay committed in the long-run? Does the goal just sound good, or is this something that you know will still be important to you a month from now?"

Timely

Goals need to be timely because they are short term in their very nature. I set three year goals and smaller goals within that. I assess my results each year and look at the activity that I am doing to drive those results.

Let's set some Goals!

How much money do you want to make this month? The first thing we need to talk about are a few key variables and the sales funnel. The best way to establish a goal is by starting from the back and working forwards. Let's say you want to make $10,000 this month. What is your average commission? $1000 per sale? Let's use that.

Leads Available: 1000 (1000/21 days= 47 calls per day) Old prospects, phone book, and people you know, names on a list, etc.

Conversion Ratio: 10% of people might be interested and qualified to present to. Right? You don't want to try to sell a Bentley to someone who is on a fixed income.

Prospects talked to: 100

Conversion Ratio: Let's say you can convince 50% of the people you speak with to set an appointment.

Appointments Set: 50

Conversion Ratio: Let's say that out of the 50 appointments you have a 50% show rate. (Which on free trials is about right.)

Presentations: 25

Closing Ratio: Of the 25 presentations you make per month you can close 50% of the presentations.

Closed Sales: 12

Average Commission: $1000

Income Projected before Chargebacks: $12,000

Chargebacks Projected: 10% of the time.

Income after Chargebacks: $11,000

Goal Reinforcement

How can you make a goal important? What I mean is that we often fall short of goals or find our sales force struggling to reach certain goals, because they're not seen as important. The foundation of goal setting is asking these two questions:

- Why am I doing this?

- Why is achieving this goal important to me?

If you do X and produce Y, why is that important? Why does it matter? What do you get out of it? If you can't answer these questions don't expect your sales team to hit their goals. Here is an example, 'Our sales team wants to write $1,000,000 in sales this month.' Who cares what you want? You do. But, does your sales team? Heck no! The first thing we need to do is give that goal some substance. Why do you want to write $1,000,000? How does it fit into your vision? How do I as an individual contributor fit into that? What will you hitting this goal do for me? Why do you want to grow? The answer may seem obvious, but if you want a goal to stick and retain importance, you'll need reinforce those goals. The 'What' doesn't matter without a compelling 'why'.

Mistakes Often Associated with Goal Setting

In this part of the chapter I'd like to spend some time talking about avoiding common misconceptions about goal setting and mistakes made during the goal setting process. Goal setting should be a rather easy task, yet many companies and people tend make the same mistakes. The most common goal setting mistakes are as follows:

- Lack of Goal Visibility

- Setting too Many Goals

- Setting Goals Too High

- Confusing a Goal for a Vision

- Setting Goals without a baseline

- Lack of Prioritization

- Losing Focus

Lack of Goal Visibility

One of the most common mistakes when setting goals is not reinforcing them by making them visible. If goals are not constantly focused on and talked about they lose all credibility. For instance, December 31st rolls around and you set a new year's resolution of losing 50 pounds, but you don't write it down. How serious is a goal if you don't even bother to write it down? For example, one day in our Rotary club we had a life insurance broker come by who actually printed his goals out on his T-shirt. Is that a bit extreme? Sure it is, but if it works then why not? For me I prefer whiteboards. Whiteboards are a great in your face way to broadcast your goals.

Setting Too Many Goals

A question I often get from new salespeople is, "How many goals should I set?" Too which I respond, "Why?" Look, you can only do so much. You can only be pulled in so many different directions. That being said, how many goals are too many goals? That answer is it depends on the person. As a new salesperson follow a simple rule, less is more. Ask yourself a simple question, "Are you spread too thin?" It's easy to get excited when setting goals, because as salespeople we are competitive people.

Setting Goals Too High

How do I know if a goal is too high? When you set a goal too high, it's almost likened to not setting a goal at all. Why? Because, if it is not achievable then why bother following through just to fail? Have you ever heard the phrase, "Rome wasn't built in a day?" Rome was built with one cobblestone at a time.

Confusing a Goal for a Vision

This is one the most basic mistakes most business people and salespeople tend to make. Growing your business to $10,000,000 is not a vision, it's a goal. Yet how many times do we see this kind of goal conflated and misrepresented as a vision. A lot of people reading this might say that all comes down to semantics, the distinction matter.

Setting Goals without a baseline

How do you know if a goal was successful? Because, you achieved it, right? Wrong. You need to know what your baseline is to establish a proper goal. For instance, let's say you in 2020 you want to sell 100 cars, or 100 insurance policies. That's a great goal, right? We don't know. How many insurance policies did you sell in 2019? What if you sold 200 in 2019? What if the year prior you sold 500? If you have no historical expectation to set a baseline, then you can always use an industry comparison or income result.

One of my favorite motivational speakers, Les Brown, will often use the example of when Roger Bannister broke the 4-minute mile. For many years it was the thinking of runners, athletes and or just the general people, that a person was incapable of running a sub-4-minute mile. This was the barrier, the impossible feat in track and field. On May 6th, 1954 Roger Bannister go on the track and shocked the world, or at least the world of track and field or the Guinness Book of World Records. The question I pose you as a reader, "Could you run a 4-minute mile?" Not a literal question, but could you in your career could you run a 4 minute mile? Maybe, yes, no? Who knows? The point is, you don't just set out to accomplish a record breaking achievement without perspective as to your ability. If you were to ask me to run a 4-minute mile, I would add ten minutes on to that time and say let's do it.

Lack of Prioritization

Prioritization is simply the process of organizing goals and ranking them by level of importance.

Guilt by Association

Associate yourself with people who can help you achieve your goals and surround yourself with people who will support you. Did you know that on average you earn within $1000 per year of your 5 closest friends? How would that change your associations?

Distracted Driving

It's easy to let things cloud our field of vision. When selling or when running a business try to avoid distractions. Social media is becoming the predominant distraction in our lives and the number one cause of auto accidents. To the point at which distracted driving has overtaken drunk driving deaths in America. When I talk about 'distracted' driving I mean it figuratively and literally. The most productive choice I ever made was to not use certain social media platforms.

"If you can't describe what you are doing as a process, you don't know what you are doing." – **Edward Deming**

Chapter 9: Selling as a Process

Chapter 9: Selling as a Process

The best piece of advice I was ever given was, "Before you can be great at something you need to learn how to be consistent at something." Simply meaning that you must master the basics before you can master the advanced aspects of your craft. In this chapter we will discuss the entirety of the sales process from opening to closing a sale. We'll examine how to design a generic sales process, how consumers interact and the boundaries we have to operate in during a sale.

What is the simplest process to emulate for a salesperson? A doctor has the best sales process. What does a doctor do? Let's think about it. You go to the Doctor for a reason; you have some uncertainty, you have an underlying worry and or some pain point. You fill out a form that more or less explains the client's concerns. Why are you here? Well, my back hurts and I don't know why. You go into a room and sit down. The doctor comes in the room with a clipboard and your pre-filled form. The doctor ask, "What brings you by today?" or something to the effect of, "What seems to be on your mind/the problem?" You explain what you think the problem is to the doctor or the reason for the visit. The doctor then using their knowledge clarifies the pain points and then figures out the problem. The doctor explains the problem and educates the patient about the problem. Why? Because, the patient has to agree there is a problem before a solution can be implemented. Now the patient has bought into the problem, the doctor presents the solution. There are usually two or three solutions. One solution involves traditional medicine, generic or name brand and or surgery. Also, maybe there are some habits that can be changed in the person's life that can solve the problem.

What will mastering a process do for me?

A lot of salespeople worry that they don't want to come off as scripted or not genuine to a prospect. Every great business uses processes. Think of McDonalds, the processes are so streamlined that a high school kid can basically run a McDonalds restaurant. Let me ask you something;

- Do you stumble into sales?

- Do you have a coherent process of how you sell?

- Are you consistently inconsistent?

Getting on Base.

When I think of selling I think of baseball. For me the best baseball camps always focused on mastering and perfecting simple processes. We we're taught to 'Squish' the bug when you pivot your foot while swinging. The big problem in professional baseball right now is that either someone hits a home run or they strike out. The big problem, demonstrated most recently by my favorite team, is lack of fundamentals. To be a good ball player, to be a good salesman for that matter, you need to learn the importance of just getting on base. The homeruns will come, don't force them, but at the same time pick up the easy base hits and eventually you will score.

Don't leap into your shtick.

It's important that you don't ambush someone with a presentation when you sell. There is a point at which you need to ask to ask for the sale. What I mean is that you ask permission to ask them for the sale.

- If I could put together some options would it be okay if we took about 20 minutes to go over them?

- Would it be okay if we talked about blank…?

Setting and Managing Expectations

Let's say you sell a service or a product. What should the client expect of you? What should you expect of a client? Every time I sat with a client I made my intentions and expectations very clear. Expectations around time, what my job was and was not, what to expect from me and what I expected from a client and how my process would benefit them. A big challenge for most new salespeople is, "How do I get referral partners to reciprocate referrals/business?" The first question I ask is, "What kind of expectations did you set?" The second question is, "What kind of follow up have you tried?" Lastly, "Are you asking for business?"

Telling isn't selling

You can spout benefits all day long until the cows come home, but for the most part consumers are going to have a hard time connecting the dots between features and price. The best way to sell a feature of a product is to determine first which features the client finds important and then convey them as benefits. For instance, in my industry follow up is king and yet so often overlooked. To set expectations with clients I would tell them a story that has happened, but might. Again, I know this sounds like common sense. But, clients may not care about what you care about. If you think X is important, they may think Y is important.

For example, telling could look something like, "What you really need is…" or "What I'd recommend for you in your situation is…" or "Based on what you told me, I'd go with BLANK to get you the lowest price." When in fact selling should involve an inquisition of some kind. For instance, "Bob, you mentioned that price was important to you. I recognize and understand that it's an important part of all our buying decisions, but what else is important to you about BLANK besides the price?" Or, "Bob I noticed that you didn't have BLANK with us, can I ask why?" Or, "Bob when was the last time you BLANK?"

What does this client care about?

People will not care about how much you know until they know how much you care. Consumers are savvy and can pick up on disingenuousness. Here are a few questions I wanted answered for every sale;

- Why are they shopping?

- What are you looking for?

- What brings you by today?

- How are their past experiences influencing their decisions?

- Besides price, what else do you care about?

- How fast are you looking to buy?

- How do you normally buy? What the process?

- How has the process been so far?

QERC Simple System

This is a system I developed and used as a salesperson. It's called the Q.E.R.C system for selling. This is a basic framework you can adhere to when selling, but don't be too rigid. Make sure to mix and match what you find useful. The process is this simple; the first step is to open with a question, the second step is to use the answer as an opportunity to educate, the third step is to make your professional recommendation and the last step is to close the sale with either a close ended or open ended question.

- **Question**
- **Educate**

- **Recommendation**

- **Close**

Question to Open: Ask an open ended question or specific question to get the conversation started. This part of the process should make up about 30-50% of your time.

Educate to flush out concerns and questions: You want to validate the problem and Segway into a solution. But, it's important that by educating the client they understand and come to agreement that a problem does in fact exist. This part of the process should make up about 10-20% of your time.

Recommendation: This is where you provide the custom tailored solution. This part of the process should make up 10-20% of your time.

Question to Close: Put the onus on the buyer to make the decision. You're an adult, they are most likely an adult, as adults we like to make up our own minds. Closing if done correctly should be quick and easy. The simplest close ended close is, "How would you like to pay?" Or for a simple open ended close, "What's getting in your way from signing up?" Closing should make up about 5-10% of your time.

The power of planting seeds

When developing your sales process it's important to know how to plant seeds. We're in the business of persuading and influencing. That can happen one of two ways, by authority or by a reciprocal exchange of ideas. Learn to ask questions and learn when to pause. The sounds of silence is a powerful tool when selling. It forces a reaction by the prospect. If you ask a question, wait for an answer.

Rapidly Identify High Intent Leads

A lot of selling depends on your ability to 'feel' out a prospect for their readiness to buy and actual intent to purchase. This can be done by gut or instinct or it can be done by directly asking questions. For instance, a simple yet powerful question such as, "How long have you been in the market for?" Or, "When do you plan on purchasing X?"

Talking in Future Tense

There is a closing strategy we will touch on later in this book called the 'Assumptive Close' or the Assumptive ask. When you ask for a sale, you ask in a way that is assumed the consumer will sign up. Prior to the close, the way to prime a consumer for that close is by speaking in future tense. What does that look like? For example, a salesperson could state, "When we're working together…" Or, "After we sign you up…" This is a great way to demonstrate tenacity and comfort with a client. When I was a trainer, I was working with a CEO of a large regional marketing firm in Los Angeles. This was during the free session, that we used for new members as a bridge to sell training sessions. I said, "John, as when we're working together a month from now…" To which he responded, "Wait a second I'm not your client yet. I haven't signed up." To which I replied, "Sure, John. You're right. If by the end of this we find that you are the right fit for me and I am the right fit for you, when we're working together a month from now…" To which, he smiled and laughed in a good way. That first hour became a three year working relationship.

Prospecting

What's the biggest problem people have when trying to prospect or network? They aren't interesting or afraid of being no interesting. Remember the old saying. "People don't care how much you know until they know how much you care?" It's that simple. Draw from that simple statement. Look if you don't know how to be interesting start by becoming interested in a person or something. Ask questions. Think about a kid who keeps asking why and the parent responds with, "Because, I said so." As a child you have this huge imagination and curiosity that gets beaten out of most people thru the 9 to 5 grind and the monotony of school. Be inquisitive and ask questions. What kind of questions? Everyone has the same favorite subject, themselves. So, ask questions about the person. People love to talk about themselves.

How many cold calls should I make per day?

The initial goal for any salesperson who is cold calling is to make as many contacts as possible. Why? The more calls you make the higher chance of getting a sale. It's really that simple. But, as a new salesperson or someone new to cold calling, there is still a learning period. You are merely getting your feed wet. As you develop your phone handling skills the goal is to increase the length of each call. The more developed your skills the less calls you will be able to make by proxy of your average conversation length increases.

Building a cold calling script

When I started in sales the first skill I had to learn was cold calling. I taught myself from scratch and let me tell you it was painstaking. The key to building a cold calling script is developing excitement by leveraging benefits and not taking a single no as a reason to quit.

- Opener: "Hi is BLANK home?"
- Who am I? My name is blank from blank.

- Ask permission to speak: Don't rush your shtick, we don't want to sell to people not qualified. Is this a good time to talk? Is this a bad time to talk? Do you have 2 minutes to go over blank?
- Quick Explanation: Explain the reason for the phone call and don't hide your purpose or bury the lead.

If you can get past this part of the conversation you have enough momentum already to build out a prospect sheet. Prospect sheet meaning enough information to set an appointment.

Here's how I learned to cold call and build a solid script:

- Identify who you are.

- Identify the reason for the call.

- Make sure to pause after asking questions.

- Don't bombard the person with features.

- Fish with some basic Benefits. The reason for the call is that...

- Ask for the sale...

Designing a Process

Every sale is the same, more or less. People tend to ask similar questions and follow similar patterns. Obviously, this is a generalization. But, people adhere to patterns and stick to certain comfort zones. People use the same objections and tend to be very consistent. Identifying these habits and patterns is the key to designing your process. Whatever you sell you basically have two options. Option one is that you can build out a cookie-cutter process, which you use but adapt for every sale. Option two is to have no process and you can stumble into sales relying mostly on instinct and guttural reaction. When building a process think of it like a guide to follow. For example, each sale starts the same way. With an interaction, with an introduction, with a greeting, etc.

Most sales people will ideally have two crucial sales appointments. A discovery call and then a subsequent presentation. This might seem like an exaggeration for some sales professions, but it depends on that industry. Typically, in my opinion, the buying process for most things is lengthy and arduous. Which means the more time you can occupy with each consumer, the higher likelihood you go home with the price. Now that being said, for some sales professions a single meeting is all you need and or want.

Theoretical Framework for a Sales Process

In this part of the book we are going to go over an example of what a sales process could look like, in theory. This is more for learning purposes and not exactly what to do.

Discovery Call (Fact Finding)

The first part of the process is the opening and discover process. We need to understand what we don't yet understand. We do this by having a consistent opening for each sale. It needs to be consistent so we can track how effective it was or wasn't. Note this isn't the exact order, play around with each part and make it your own.

Opening

An opening should be focused on three things; establish rapport, set expectations and get the client thinking. Here are some sample questions to try out;

- "What brings you by today?"
- "How can we help?"

From there you can set expectations. Which could look something like, 'As your salesperson (insert title), my job is to help you with blank. If at any point in the process you have questions, please feel free to ask away. Now, that being said, before we get started with process, what kind of questions do you have about your BLANK?'

Rapport Building

An easy rapport building strategy can be as simple as three or four questions.

- What do you do for a living?
- How long have you been doing that?
- What do you enjoy about it?
- Why did you chose to be a BLANK?

Address Questions and Concerns

Salesperson: "Before we get started what kind of questions or concerns do you have?"
Prospect: Isn't it true that BLANK...
Salesperson: "That's interesting you would say that, why do you ask?"

Fact Finding

During the fact finding process you want to accomplish two things. You want to do the functional fact finding which means finding out if the buyer is qualified and also find out what they really are looking to do.

- "What would you change about your current BLANK?"

- "When was the last time you reviewed your BLANK?"
- "Do you think you have enough BLANK?"
- "I noticed that you don't have BLANK, can I ask why?"
- "Besides price, what do you care about?"
- "How long have you been shopping for BLANK? What has that experience been like?"

Along with that we want to; Determine goals, evaluate current situation, determine a problem (if any), and see how we can help.

Problem Identification

Problem identification is the cornerstone of your presentation. Why? Because, people are coming to you to solve a problem. Problem identification should be woven into the entire process.

- I'm a little worried with your current level of blank.
- 'I noticed you had blank but not blank, who would that currently be with now?'
- As we begin to work on some options, would it be okay if we looked at BLANK as well? I didn't

see it in your current paperwork. Do you know who you have that with now?

- I see that your BLANK is at BLANK, can I ask how you arrived at that number?
- Did you have a specific BLANK in mind or were you looking for some guidance?

All these questions should be built into your needs analysis and part of the process.

Commitment to Close

Ask for permission to ask for the close. For example, 'What I'd like to do now is spend about 15 minutes going over some potential options. How does that sound?' Or, "If I could work up some numbers, would you be willing to give me about 10 minutes of your time to cover possible solutions?" You don't want to ambush someone with your presentation or not let them know you are about to close them on something. Think about it like how rude it is to open someone else's refrigerator without asking for permission.

Sales Call (Presentation)

There are numerous styles of sales presentations. In this part of the book I'm going to walk through the 5 most common strategies. The five strategies are;

- Single Solution Presentation
- Three Solution Presentation
- Single High Cost Offer with a back Up Low Cost
- Apples to Apples Presentation
- Apples to Oranges Presentation

The first strategy is the most popular, which is the 'Single Solution Presentation Strategy'. The single solution strategy is rather simple, it's a method in which you present just a single option. Easy, right? What's the risk? The risk is that it's a take it or leave it proposal.

The second most popular method is the "Three Option Presentation". Think of this method like a tiered or pyramid approach. You have the most expensive option at the top, a middle option and a lower end lower cost option at the bottom of the pyramid. This method is where you let the prospect chose between the three, and most people choose the middle option.

Another option is called, "The Single Option High Cost with Low Cost back-up" I'm always a big fan of having a Plan B in place, in case Plan A doesn't pan out. This approach is a fishing line approach, you throw out a line and hope for the best knowing you have a lower cost fall back. This method is great for earning additional income with very little added work. This was my approach when selling, and it worked quite well.

The fourth option is an Apples to Apples style comparison. When someone has X you present your version of X. The challenge here is that without an existing relationship there is minimal value transference to the client.

Lastly I want to talk about the Apples to Orange presentation strategy. This is a strategy that customizes an offering for a client. For instance, the client has X and you present Y.

Identifying Buying Questions

Selling is both an art and a science. It's an art form because of things like buying questions and the influence over the process. You could follow some immaculate and elaborate sales process, but it could all be ruined if you ignore buying questions. What are buying questions? Buying questions are a sign of a client ready to buy. They are process questions. Such as;

- How much does something like this cost?
- Do you take AMEX?
- Do you split up payments?
- How would I get started with something like that?

Closing Strategies

The simplest closes are the most effective. Closes can be either open ended or close ended. The most common closing strategies include;

- Take-Away Close
- Assumptive Close
- Trial Close
- Option Close (Tiered Offering)

The key to closing is using a simple formula. Use your close, shut up and wait for an answer.

But Mike, I don't want to come off as phony by using a standard process...

You're asking the same questions every sale. There are qualifying questions you have to ask to close a sale. Just put it into a work flow. Don't worry about being phony, worry more about be looked at as unprofessional. Pros have a system and they have a process. It's as simple as that.

Asking for referrals

I'm going to take somewhat of a controversial stance here and claim that asking for referrals is the easiest possible way to grow your business. One of the most common questions I get from salespeople is not if but, 'When should do I ask for referrals?' Should you ask before the sale or after the sale? In my opinion, you should ask before the sale. You should ask when the topic is top of mind. How often do you get referrals when you ask post sale? Exactly, not often enough. An easy way to ask is, "Do you have any friends, family, neighbors or co-workers that might be struggling with their BLANK?" Or, "Do you have any X, Y and Z that you think could use my help with BLANK?"

Filler Questions

Sometimes during the sales process not everything goes smoothly. For example, a computer can crash and cause a lot of awkward silence while you scramble to fix it. Or we have some 'down time' during the actual presentation where we need to fill a gap. So, come prepared with some rapport based filler questions.

Check the Rapport

Selling is a lot like cooking a turkey. There is a very specific process for cooking a turkey, without completely ruining the turkey. The first step is that you have to de-thaw the turkey or you ruin it. You have to pre-heat the oven or you could ruin the turkey. You have to baste the turkey, or you ruin it. You have to know how many hours per pound to cook it. You have to check the temperature every so often, or you ruin it. With rapport building, it's not a one and done exercise. You have to check the rapport just like you would the temperature on a turkey.

- "Does this all make sense so far?"

- "How does this all sound so far?"

- "What kind of questions do you have?"

The reason why this is so important is to make sure that you don't ambush the prospect prior to the close/presentation. To quote one of my favorite Chris Tucker movies, "Do you understand the words coming out of my mouth?" The key to checking rapport is checking that the client understands you, the concept and what they are buying. Because, the last thing you want to do is guess if they are going to buy or not.

Why you need a process, now!

Enthusiasm is not a process. Hoping people will buy your product or hoping people will like you enough to buy is not a process. I'm not saying to be unlikable or don't be enthusiastic. I'm saying if you don't stick to a consistent process, you'll be stuck flying by the seat of your pants.

AIDA – Attention, Interest, Decision and Action.

Remember, AIDA? AIDA is an old sales mantra that was prevalent in the 1980's sales training vernacular. It stands for; Attention, Interest, Decision and Action. It's what I based my entire selling system on. But, how do we execute that? Q.E.R.C or Open, Educate, Recommend and Close.

Opener – the best way to get someone's attention is with a provocative question, an interesting statement and or something that challenges an ideal. Use an attention grabber. For instance, did you know that 60% of people at under-insured by at least 22%? That's a real stat and if you own a home could mean financial ruin.

Educate – Every time you ask a question it opens up opportunities. Identify opportunities and problems/challenges facing customer. Get customer to buy into problem. When we can educate we empower consumers to help them make informed purchasing decisions.

Recommend – Explain the solution and make a professional recommendation.

Close – Ask a question and close. If you are presenting value, closing is easy. If you neglect a proper needs analysis, closing is often an uphill battle. A good close puts the onus on the buyer (who is now properly informed) to make a decision.

Sales Management – Designing a Lead Workflow / Sales Process

As a sales manager figure out what your lead process looks like. Start by asking yourself and your staff a few key questions. Such as;

- When a lead comes in, how is it distributed?

- What is the call back time from the initial distribution of the lead?

- Is there an automated callback, text and or email set up?

- What questions are being asked to qualify the lead prior to contact by the salesperson?

- What percentage of the leads are actually real? (Fake phone numbers, not genuine, etc.)

- How many attempts were made to contact the lead?

- How are you documenting the reasons for leads not sold and the close ratio per competition business?

- How are leads coming in? What sources?

Time Decay when working leads

When designing your lead system one of your key indicators of success is time decay. The longer the lead sits without a contact the more likely the shopper moves on. Simple, right? The Harvard business review ran a study to understand business lead responsiveness and time decay.

The take away from this is that about 37% of companies only respond within an hour of the lead submission. When you purchase or work an online lead, you have a very-very short time to call back. Some estimates on lead decay are 20 to 30 minutes, before a lead is rendered worthless.

What most Sales Processes look like, when you ask salespeople.

When I train salespeople one of my favorite trainings is helping people develop a consistent process. I'll have them take out a piece of paper and ask them to draw a process.

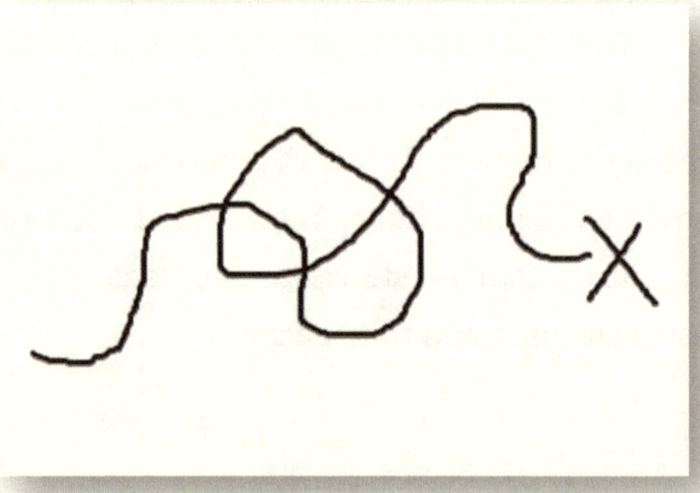

The next part of that exercise is to list out all the questions you ask and the order in which you ask them, more or less. Your sales process should be ingrained into your brain.

- What do you say if someone says they do not have time?
- What do you say if someone says they are not interested?
- What do you say if someone says that they don't know you?

Most salespeople sort of have a process, but more or less stumble into each close and vary wildly in their process, which is almost like not having a process.

Every Sale is the same, more or less.

Every sale is the same, more or less. What I mean by that, is that our process for every sale should be more or less the same. Otherwise how do we know when it works or fails? The questions we ask to qualify an account should have a repeatable order. When we pause… and for how long we pause… should be more or less the same. The sale has a starting line and a finish line.

Confidence is Key

Confidence also comes in to play with core leadership and sales principles. In the 2nd grade I was forced into acting in a school play. After some hesitation and nerves, the acting teacher told me, "Look the audience won't know if you screw up, unless you show them or tell them you screwed up. So, if you forget your lines, make it up and fake it until you make it." When we are presenting or qualifying, be confident. People want to be around confident people and more importantly we want to follow confident people who have the 'answers'.

Principle of Exclusivity

Things that are plentiful and abundant have little value compared to things that are scare. When something is exclusive, it holds a higher value. If your product is something that requires qualification, there is value. Remember, not every customer is a customer. This as a salesperson was a hard concept for me to grasp. You need to be selective, not everyone that walks in the door is going to be an ideal fit for your service or product.

Principle of Urgency

A good salesperson knows how to create a sense of urgency in the prospect.

Principle of Reciprocity

The rule of reciprocity is rather simple. If I give there is an expectation that I get in return. So, if I spend time listening to your problems as a consumer, the idea is that there is an implied social arrangement that you will give me some time to listen to my sales pitch? Otherwise known as give before you get, but get something in return.

Customize Your Offering and Approach

Consumers want a customized solution over a bland solution. The more you can customize your offering and approach, the easier time you will have selling your product or services. A customized offer allows you to really fit the product/service to the specific need of your customer.

Generate Some Excitement

Learn to be excitable and get the prospect excited for what they're buying. I know this is going to sound like common sense, but make buying from you an enjoyable experience.

Recommendation + Reason = More Sale

The easiest way for novice sales people to improve their close ratio is by attaching reasons to their recommendations. Compliance studies show that strangers will agree to your requests, if you provide reasons with the request. Psychologist Ellen Langer ran a now famous study to prove this concept. In the study a participant would find a photocopier in which a line had formed. The participant would go to the front of the line and ask to effectively cut in line. Asking alone will produce a result. Asking with a reason produces a much greater effective result.

Version 1 (request only): "Excuse me, I have 5 pages. May I use the Xerox machine?"

Version 2 (request with a real reason): "Excuse me, I have 5 pages. May I use the Xerox machine, because I'm in a rush?"

Version 3 (request with a fake reason): "Excuse me, I have 5 pages. May I use the Xerox machine, because I have to make copies?"

Version 1: 60 percent of people let the researcher skip the line.

Version 2: 94 percent of people let the researcher skip ahead in line.

Version 3: 93 percent of people let the researcher skip ahead in line.

Asking Permission to Ask for the Sale

Would you mind if we spent some time and spoke about... Would it be okay if we spoke about...? What I've found from working with middle class families is that... Now that we have a precise idea of what you're looking for, would it be okay if we sat down to talk about some options? Don't just force a conversation or close on someone.

Asking for the sale

When closing... use simple closes to seal the deal. How would you like to pay? And pause... and wait for an answer. With closing the first person to speak loses. Wait for that answer and go from there. I'm still shocked by how many salespeople I encounter that do not directly ask for the sale. Your intention every time you sit down with a qualified client should be acquisition and let them know that. If you're a good fit for my firm, I'd be happy to help you out. I'd like to work with you... how hard is that? Don't dance around what you want.

Don't talk yourself out of a sale...

Sometimes you don't need to go thru your entire presentation to close a deal out. Think of agreeableness like a standard bell curve. Some people on the left side of the curve agree instantly and some on the right side of the curve take a while to come around. Some consumers are easy to close and some are hard to close, it's that simple.

How do I identify buying signals and buying questions?

Buying questions and signals are indications that the prospect is ready to be closed, but maybe has some process questions before taking ownership. When I work with new salespeople or existing salespeople I often ask, "What are buying questions?" When do you know a consumer is ready to buy? Here are some examples of buying questions:

- What kind of financing options do you provide/have?
- Does it have to come with X? Or can I get it without X?
- What other colors does that come in?
- How long does it take to sign up? (Remember take care of all the heavy lifting or perception)

- Do you have any referrals or customer testimonials you can share? Do you work with other vendors in my area?
- Would this work with my current setup/system?
- How much time/money could it save my company/me?
- Do I qualify for any other discounts?
- How quickly can we start/how long would it take us to set this up?
- What do we need to do on our end to set this up?
- Can I finance it? Thru your shop? If so, how much would it cost?

Analysis Paralysis

Ever have a client ask, "What are my options?" That can be a Pandora's Box of potential answers. What clients are really looking for is pin-pointed specific laser focused customized solutions and a close. Don't throw so much information at a prospect that they become paralyzed with the information to analyze.

Don't Sell to Un-qualified Buyers

Not everyone is a customer! Some prospects are not meant to buy your product. Don't try to force your product/service on someone who is not qualified. For ethical reasons yes, but also because you are wasting the customer's time and wasting your own time.

Focus the Conversation

As a salesperson the most effective messaging we can craft focuses the conversation on the end user. Whether marketing or selling, consumers are people and people have limited attention spans. Along with the fact consumers are constantly bombarded with information. In a typical sales presentation how many benefits do you want to illuminate to a consumer? How many concepts are too many concepts to discuss?

For example, an insurance contract has anywhere from 10 to 100 features and benefits to a consumer. How do you know which ones to pick out and explain? Start by explaining the benefits the consumer cares about and the features that matter. No matter how good of a salesperson, don't get offended when consumers might forget a piece of information that you explained two minutes ago. The reason why we have to focus the conversation is that every person falls prey to **Short Term Memory. Short Term Memory** can be defined by three key aspects; limited capacity, limited duration of recall and encoding. Short term memory seems to be somewhere between 15 to 30 seconds.

Displacement from Short Term Memory

Displacement: seeks to explain forgetting in short term memory, and suggests that forgetting is due to a lack of availability. **Displacement theory** suggests that a typical person can recall anywhere from 5 to 9 pieces of information in their short term memory, because Miller suggests that a person has a very limited capacity to hold small amounts of information. Displacement also implies or assumes that the piece of information that was stored for the longest is the first to be replaced. Think of it like FIFO accounting, or first in first out. If you explain 10 concepts in sequential order, the 10th concept might very well replace the 1st concept in a consumer's available memory to recall.

Fictional Example

When I read this section (see below) in Sherlock Holmes it opened my mind to the value of selective learning and displacement theory. This section was pulled from *A Study in Scarlet*. "You see," he explained, "I consider that a man's brain originally is like a little empty attic, and you have to stock it with such furniture as you choose. A fool takes in all the lumber of every sort that he comes across, so that the knowledge which might be useful to him gets crowded out, or at best is jumbled up with a lot of other things so that he has a difficulty in laying his hands upon it. Now the skillful workman is very careful indeed as to what he takes into his brain-attic. He will have nothing but the tools which may help him in doing his work, but of these he has a large assortment, and all in the most perfect order. It is a mistake to think that that little room has elastic walls and can distend to any extent. Depend upon it there comes a time when for every addition of knowledge you forget something that you knew before. It is of the highest importance, therefore, not to have useless facts elbowing out the useful ones."

"A good plan violently executed now is better than a
perfect plan executed next week." George S. Patton

Chapter **10: Fact Finder**

Chapter 10: Fact Finder

In this chapter we are going to discuss one of the most overlooked parts of a salespersons toolkit, a fact finder. We're going to talk about what a fact finder can do, how it can help, how to develop a fact finder, the necessity of when to use a fact finder in conjunction with your sales process, common mistakes of a fact finder and the key elements for fact finder design.

What is a fact finder? A **Fact Finder** is just a simple needs analysis tool, usually just a piece of paper. What makes a good fact finder? Let me ask you something. How do you gather information to prepare a quote/proposal/estimate? What variables do you collect during your discovery process? Let me ask you another question. How often do you ever think about revising your fact finder?

Three Core Elements of a Fact Finder

In theory a proper fact finder can cover many topics. That being said in my opinion a great fact finder has 3 core components.

- Where have you been?

- Where are you now?

- Where do you want to go?

Where have you been?

So, let's break that down and be a little more specific. Here are some questions that should be answered in a fact finder, not literally but from an understanding perspective.

- Why is that person in front of you?
- Why are they interested?
- What unmet concern or question do they have?
- What are the customers past experiences buying an X?
- Do they not have an experience buying an X?

That might be valuable information for you to know! This also allows you to discover some pain points. **Pain points** according to Jeffrey Carter can be defined as, "A pain point is a problem, real or perceived." History is often very revealing. In that history can reveal preconceived notions the consumer may hold, perceptions, beliefs, experiences, etc.

Where are you now?

Would it benefit you to know that your customer's financial situation has recently changed? Would it benefit you to know that a prospect is worried about their current financial situation? And would it benefit you to know why? Are you on track? Why are you sitting in front of me right now? Why are we talking?

Where do you want to go?

What are your goals? What does the client want to accomplish by speaking with you? What does a prospect want to achieve? Why is this person talking to me?

Purpose of a Fact Finder

A fact finder is a great tool for new or beginning sales people to keep you on track. What a fact finder does is focus the conversation and will give you some structure. A fact finder will help you gather facts so you can customize a proposal and analyze the current situation of a client. As you grow more experiences as a salesperson you will most likely not need a fact finder. Here are three reasons why you might want a fact finder:

1. **Errors and Omissions** Protection

2. Helps Focus the Conversation

3. Helps gather all relevant information needed for a quote

Errors and Omissions

If you're not familiar with E&O, it's a type of insurance for professionals who give advice or forget to give advice. Most salespeople have some form of Errors and Omissions protection. Why? Because, sometimes in our profession claims are made against us for making errors or omitting information that might have been relevant to a client prior to purchase.

Focus

Focusing the conversation is extremely important because, one we have limited time with a consumer, two we want to stay on track and three as salespeople we need to remember there is a reason why the other person is sitting across from us.

Memory and Fact Gathering

How many pieces of information can you remember in your head about every single transaction or prospecting call? Having a fact finder will for the most part ensure we do not forget to ask certain relevant questions. This reduces the need to go back to the prospect and re-ask for information we may have forgotten.

Mistakes of Most Fact Finders

A fact finder is not about solutions, the purpose of a fact finder is to just gather information, uncover needs and discover pain points. It's meant to provide you with information so you can take some time and actually come up with a proper solution that is tailor made to fit the needs of the client. How you start a fact finder is incredibly important. When I work on this with salespeople I often look at fact finders that are purely analytical in nature or for underwriting purposes. For one of my more recent meetings I was sitting in the lobby of an office and happened to see a fact finder on the front desk. Over 90% of the information was purely bland underwriting-data driven. It didn't tell me anything about the person and didn't express anything about the motivations of why the person was looking to purchase. A brighter note at the bottom of the fact finder there was at least, "How did you hear about us?" To which I asked, "Why isn't that question at the top of the sheet?"

Some Fact Finder Questions

Here are some great questions to think about integrating into your fact finder?

- What does this person care about besides price?

- How'd they hear about us?

- Preferred communication style? Do you prefer text, email, phone, face to face?

- Follow Up Day or Night

- Follow Up Date

- Occupation

- What does your current offering look like? (Generic, make it specific)

- Is your current plan underperforming, meeting and or exceeding your expectations?

- How often would you like follow ups (check-ups)? Yearly, semi-annually, monthly, etc. (Referring to follow ups after signing a client)

"The whole is more than the sum of its parts." – Aristotle

Chapter 11: Closing a Sale

Chapter 11: Closing a Sale

In this chapter we are going to discuss the art of closing. **Closing** simply defined is the final step of a sales process where we attempt to convert the prospect into a client. Closing if done correctly should be short and to the point. Closing is where most novice sales people tend to spend the majority of their time. If you front load the sales process, closing should be simple and easy. If you rush the needs analysis, product explanation and forgo the rapport process, closing becomes much more of an uphill battle.

Asking to Ask Asking for permission to ask for the sale.

When I audit sales calls for quality assurance, I can't tell you how many times asking for permission to ask for the sale goes obliviously overlooked by the salesperson. What do I mean by asking for permission to ask for the sale? Growing up I was always taught to never open another person's refrigerator without asking for permission first. The last thing people want to endure is a pseudo consensual sales presentation. Most salespeople pivot from a concept right into asking for the sale. How rude is that? Think about it from the perspective of a consumer. You're looking at a car and the sales rushes eagerly right into the close. Is it really that hard to say, "Great now that we have a rough idea of what you want, what I'd like to is sit down and look at some options to help you out, how does that sound?"

Three Most Common Closing Questions

- When do I know a person is ready to be closed?
- When should I close?

- How do I close a sale?

When do I know a person is ready to be closed?

What do we mean by this? Some prospects are easier to close than others. Some prospects want a short conversation and some a lengthier conversation. Some prospects you can spend a minimal amount of time with and present a price and some it takes a full presentation and some follow up after the presentation. This all gets back to identifying buying questions and being able to read body language.

When should I close?

Although we talk about having a process, sometimes prospects can be closed by just asking at the onset of the conversation. Some prospects don't have questions and they know what they want to buy. This is where the 'art' of sales comes into play and experience impacts the outcomes of the sale. Often a feeler close can be put out there at the onset, "Well it sounds like you're ready to buy now… all we need is a credit card to get you started…" Sometimes it works.

How do I close a sale?

Closing is not some mystical and mysterious secret, although as a salesman I would like to think there is some mystique to the process. Closing is as simple or as complex a process as you want to make of it. How do you close a sale? You ask with intent, confidence and purpose. Then you shut up and wait for an answer. One of the biggest mistakes I see new salespeople making is not asking for the sale. A lot of people end up getting so nervous, they forget to ask or purposely do not ask.

How do I determine my Close Ratio?

First we need to determine how many people you speak with per month. For example, if you make 1000 phone calls per month and are able to convince 100 people to hear your presentation you are converting 10% of leads into presentations. Among those 100 people typically speaking 50% (if **cold leads**) will show up to the presentation. This is known as your '**show rate**' or how many appointments are held compared to scheduled appointments. So, 50 prospects sit for a presentation, how many can we close? Let's say of those 50 presentations we close 25% of them or 12 new customers.

Closing Strategies

Closing strategies do not work in a vacuum. You must understand the prospect and understand how much wiggle room you have during the sales process. One closing strategy might not work for all clients. Picking a closing strategy is like picking a style. It's something you have to be comfortable and confident with all the time, it has to empower you and the consumer. The simple the closing strategy the better, why? Because, we don't want to confuse the consumer into purchasing, because it's unethical and will lead to a lot of chargebacks.

- Take Away Close (Exclusivity) – Pull the proposal back. This is a powerful psychological subliminal demonstration during the sale demonstrating the power dynamic. The prospect is pushing back a little bit and pulling back so we mirror and physically pull back the offer from even being purchased.
- Assumptive Close - How would you like to pay for that?

Options after the Close.

At the end of the sale we have the opportunity to close the sale. Now at this point one of two things can happen. Either we close the sale and acquire the client or we don't. If client acquisition has failed we now have the opportunity to put the client back into the lead funnel. This allows us the opportunity to Follow-up with the prospect.

"Just because you're doing a lot more doesn't mean you're getting a lot more done." –Denzel Washington

Chapter 12: Follow Up

Chapter 12: Follow Up

In this chapter we are going to talk about Follow-Up. **Follow-Up** is the simple process of re-contacting a previous prospect who we did not convert into a customer. Follow up systems if done correctly should be simple and allow for opt-out.

Follow Up Systems

Many Customer Relationship Management (CRM) programs have automated follow-up otherwise known as **'drip' systems**. Every industry is slightly different in regards to compliance issues with these campaigns. As a tool a drip system can drastically increase your sales count and overall efficiency as a salesperson. Developing and designing proper follow up systems can be the difference maker for maintaining and cultivating an active sales funnel.

The three types of follow up systems we will focus on are:

- Lead management
- Client Renewals
- Prospect Did Not Sell (DNS)

Lead Management

Lead management follow up systems are crucial to the top end development of your sales funnel. When a lead comes in, what do you do? The answer is you shouldn't have to think about the process. There should be an exact process to lead follow up from, how you contact the prospect to how fast you contact the prospect.

Client Renewal Programs

If your profession relies on clients re-upping or renewing a service/product, then renewal programs are your most important list to work each day. Don't take this renewals for granted.

Prospect Did Not Sell (DNS)

Every time you don't sell an account. What happens to that prospect? You put them right back up from the bottom of the sales funnel to the top of the funnel. When do you contact a DNS lead? How often do you contact a DNS lead?

Designing a Follow-Up Process

Designing an effective follow up system requires us to look at many different variables.

- When is the best time to call?

- When is the prospects preferred call back time/day?

- How does the prospect want to be contacted? Email/Text/Call

- Does your email template have a **squeeze page**?

- Do you have an email template that you can consistently use?

- How much time can you dedicate to **Call-Backs**?

- Are you able to track **open-rates** and **click-thru-rates (CTR)**?

An effective Follow-Up system relies on your understanding of the above variables.

https://www.leadsimple.com/sales-course/follow-up-tactics

"Ethics is knowing the difference between what you have a right to do and what is right to do." –Potter Stewart

Chapter 13: Sales Ethics

Sales Ethics

In this chapter we are going to discuss Sales Ethics. Ethical decision making should be the lens in which you view selling. That being said we are going to talk about the questions you should be considering for each sale and how it effects your sales process. As you develop your career in selling and become more experienced the stakes can become higher and the risk to the customer can increase. As salespeople we work in an industry where credibility and reputation are paramount to our success. Information has been proliferated and has become easily widespread. In this modern era of information sharing consumer rating sites can single handedly destroy a business.

Developing a Code of Ethics

How do we build a code of ethics? As salespeople or as sales managers we need to clearly define and communicate our code of ethics. How do we develop a culture of ethical thinking and ethical selling? Simple, we focus on a simple old mantra, "Say what you mean, mean what you say and do what you say you'll do." As you develop your code of ethics or code of conduct, write your principles down with the customer in mind. When I drafted my original code of ethics I wrote down a simple question, "Would I be okay selling this product to my mother, my sisters and my grandmother?" It's a simple qualification for me to make correct and honorable decisions.

Core Components of Ethical Selling

- Transparent Communication

- Product Review and Comparison

- Focus on Educating the client

- If I were in the customer's position, would I buy?

* Focus on Qualification over Closing

* Build a culture of development and education

* Reduce or eliminate conflicts of interest

* Show the customer we care

Ethical Lens

If you were to qualify each of your statements during a sales presentation, what would that qualifying question be? In my opinion that question would be:

* Is this customer qualified to buy this product?

If the answer to this question is yes, then pitch it. If the answer to this question is no, then don't pitch it. As a rule of thumb, never pitch to an unqualified buyer. Why? So, we can avoid buyer's remorse. So, we can avoid bad reviews or negative publicity. So, we can avoid chargebacks. So, we can build a culture of referrals and promote goodwill. So, we do not inadvertently damage our brand. Most of the time we can use our judgement for what is and isn't ethical. If you have to ask if it's ethical, then you're probably dealing with an unethical issue.

Ethical Decision Making: How do I know?

How do I know if an action is ethical or not? If an action is illegal by its nature the action is unethical. For legal actions that are questionable, a grey area. Make sure to consult an attorney. The best way to get a specific answer would be to ask your sales manager or compliance department. There is no one size fits all approach to ethics, ultimately we have to be okay with decisions we make.

Summation

Thanks for taking the time to read my book. I'd like to leave you with three key takeaways:

1. Be Emotional about the concept you are selling and logical about the process.

2. Don't confuse activity for productivity.

3. Don't disregard effectiveness in the pursuit of perfection. Because, by the time your plan is in perfect order it might no longer be effective.

I've always enjoyed selling and more over helping people learn how to sell. Selling is the ultimate test of your endurance. When the sales slumps come, and they will come, don't forget that selling doesn't have to be cyclical. Focus on what you can control in the process. Focus on what you can do differently to add value. Focus on how you can improve your pitch or qualification process. Most importantly of all, don't get discouraged and don't be afraid to fail. If you are struggling, double your efforts. If you are struggling keep investing in your mind because education is the one thing in life that no one can take away from you. Keep reading and keep talking to people. Talk to enough people and say the right things.

Index of Questions

Rapport and Prospecting Questions:

- What do you do for a living?

- How long have you been doing that for?

- How'd you get involved in that activity/hobby?

- What do you like about it?

- Why did you get involved in that?

- Was that something your family has been doing for a while or something you thought to strike out on your own and do?

- What do you do really well?

Opening Questions:

- What brings you by today?

- How'd you hear about us?

- How can we help?

- Thanks for coming in today. Before we get started what kind of questions or concerns did you have?

Qualifying Questions:

- How long have you been in the market for BLANK?

- How many BLANKs have you looked at so far?

    o What's your experience been like so far?

- Is it important to you to have after-hours or weekend service?

- Besides price, what's important to you?

    o What else is important?

        ▪ Why?

- Have you ever owned a BLANK in the past?

    o What was that experience like?

- I noticed you didn't have BLANK, why is that?

- Would you mind if we talked about BLANK?

Clarifying Questions:

- Does that make sense?

- Does this all make sense so far?

- Did you have an idea of what you were looking for? Or did you need some guidance?

- Would you consider paying slightly more for your BLANK, if I could get you BLANK?

- When was the last time you sat down with your BLANK expert and reviewed your BLANK?

- What does your ideal plan look like?

Closing Questions:
- How would you like to pay?

Introspective Questions – Quality Assurance Questions
- Why am I doing this?

- If I were a customer, what would I want to know?

- What's in it for them?

- What value am I providing?

- Why should a consumer buy from me and not the guy down the street?

Buying Questions
- How much does something like that cost?

- What would it cost me?

- Can I pay in chunks or do I have to pay all at once?

- What kind of financing options do you provide/have?

- Does it have to come with X? Or can I get it without X?

- What other colors does that come in?

- How long does it take to sign up? (Remember take care of all the heavy lifting or perception)

- Do you have any referrals or customer testimonials you can share? Do you work with other vendors in my area?

- Would this work with my current setup/system?

- How much time/money could it save my company/me?

- Do I qualify for any other discounts?

- How quickly can we start/how long would it take us to set this up?

- What do we need to do on our end to set this up?

- Can I finance it? Thru your shop? If so, how much would it cost?

www.ingramcontent.com/pod-product-compliance
Lightning Source LLC
Chambersburg PA
CBHW020906160726
47993CB00005B/1833